Living The Mystery of Merciful Love

30 days with Thérèse of Lisieux

Living The Mystery of Merciful Love

30 days with Thérèse of Lisieux

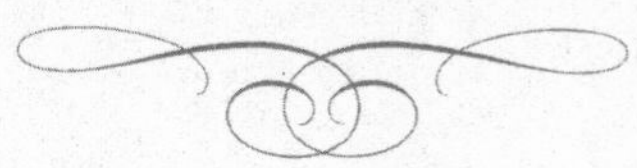

WITH AN INTRODUCTION AND REFLECTIONS BY
ANTHONY LILLES AND DAN BURKE

Living the Mystery of Merciful Love was previously published by Emmaus Road Publishing, 827 North Fourth Street, Steubenville, Ohio 43952.

Original cover design by Claudia Volkman.
Cover and interior layout by Margaret Ryland.
Printed in the United States of America.

Sophia Institute Press
Box 5284, Manchester, NH 03108
1-800-888-9344

www.SophiaInstitute.com

Sophia Institute Press® is a registered trademark of Sophia Institute.

TABLE OF CONTENTS

INTRODUCTION

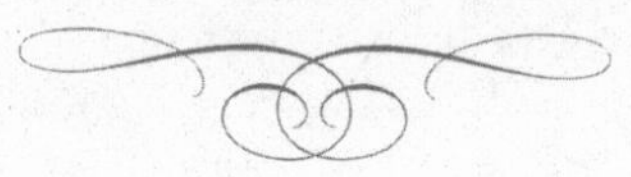

You have in your hands a thirty-day retreat that can—and will—change your life. We don't propose that you spend thirty days off in a cave somewhere. That would be contrary to the spirit of St. Thérèse. Instead, we propose that for thirty days you invite God into the midst of your daily toil and that through the wisdom of St. Thérèse you explore the ways that He desires to meet you in your daily life and in your toil and lead you to heaven through it.

The Act of Oblation to Merciful Love and excerpts of twenty-nine letters authored by St. Thérèse of Lisieux are arranged here for thirty day-by-day meditations. This spiritual exercise intends to prepare you to renew the Act of Oblation to Merciful Love each day. At the end of this retreat, our hope is that this daily self-offering will have become an integral part of your personal prayer and that your heart will discover the dynamism of Divine Mercy.

True devotion is fed by truth. To this end, each one of our thirty meditations brings out a slightly different aspect of the Act of Oblation for consideration and prayer. As we proceed, the beautiful horizons of mercy that Thérèse shared with her contemporaries can become our own. This effort is not merely a mental exercise. The instruction provided in these pages presumes that the battle for the heart is waged in the mind. We seek in St. Thérèse's spiritual teaching a deeper and more personal encounter with God. Her own words to her closest family members and friends provide the mystagogical content—the spiritual catechesis—for these reflections. We simply provide theological context and highlight autobiographical details that draw out the implications of her teachings. By allowing her to draw you into the beautiful horizons that she invited her friends and family to share, she will prepare you to imitate her as she imitated Christ—by offering yourself for love, by love, and with love.

What is an Oblation? An oblation is an act of giving oneself to God for a sacred purpose. To be an oblation to the Merciful Love of God means to offer one's own life to God so that through it His Mercy might be revealed. An oblation is more than a momentary act of devotion or a one-time event. It is a total life commitment. The offering is meant to become a spiritual heartbeat that carries us through the day, and one that we renew at every opportunity.

St. Thérèse understood her daily oblation as a pathway to sanctity. For her, it was more than a recitation of words on a page. It outlined a whole discipline of life. She makes her Oblation to Merciful Love because she wants to be a saint. Her self-offering is intended to be nothing other than a participation in Christ's holiness for the salvation of the world. If Thérèse's oblation is ultimately ordered to the holiness of God, she also offers it for a more immediate purpose: namely, to live one single act with perfect love.

She offers herself to Merciful Love because she wants to show her love in action, by love and for love alone. St. Thérèse is well aware of her own mixed motives and inadequacies, yet these are not the focus of her oblation. Instead, her offering focuses on the God who can bring to perfection the work that He has begun if only souls surrender to Him and makes space for His love. To make the Oblation is to commit oneself to this divine project. Such an offering requires great courage and determination, but more than that, it requires confidence in and passion for the Mercy of God.

Introduction

Mercy is love pierced to the heart by the plight of another. Within the logic of mercy, a perfect act of love is offered when nothing holds us back from our effort to remove the misery of our neighbor and affirm his or her dignity. Devotion to Divine Mercy recognizes how God's excessive love for us has moved Him to relieve the disgrace and alienation that our sin has brought into our lives.

In this devotion, St. Thérèse is deeply moved by a profound mystery. She knows that in God's omnipotence and authority over all, He knows perfectly the depths of human misery and the mystery of evil. God's perfection cannot block the perfect tenderness and compassion that He offers to humanity. But unless we freely avail ourselves of this unfathomable love, He cannot force us to receive it. Here, we begin to glimpse the immense mystery that engulfs the existence of St. Thérèse like a drop lost in an ocean. In between the tenderness that God yearns to show broken humanity and the mystery of freedom with which He endows each person, Thérèse recognizes a kind of divine anguish: a love that yearns to be shared but is in a sense frustrated until it is freely accepted. The distress that she perceives does not pose a weakness in God, but rather the dramatic proportion of His perfect love for humanity.

These insights into the merciful love of God help us understand the importance that St. Thérèse places on the oblation in her own time. After the Prussian occupation in the nineteenth century, many believed that God had abandoned France because France had abandoned God. Indeed, with the Industrial Revolution and the rise of secularism, the rich blessings of the faith, once dominant in European culture, were now diminished. Instead, preoccupation with material success and political ideologies defined the self-perception of the people and dictated the way they spent their time. An old fashioned and moralizing Church seemed to be out of touch with their daily concerns. Ecclesial indifference or even defensiveness concerning the pressures of modern life only confirmed these popular impressions.

Among many of the devout, there was a desire to rectify France's standing with God. Some religious offered themselves to divine justice in an effort to make reparation for the sins of their countrymen against God. Their effort was to bridge the gap between the demands of divine justice and the mediocre piety of their contemporaries by making sensational penitential acts and sacrifices on behalf of the ungodly. Over and against this effort, St. Thérèse explicitly acknowledges that she was not capable of this kind of spiritual feat. She seems to have intuited a hubris inherent to this approach that lacked an authentic spirit of reparation and intercession. The problem was not that the world was unjust or filled with misery—it tragically was and even more tragically is today. Her saintly genius was to see the problem instead as a lack of humble openness in the Church to the graces that God yearned to give.

Some attempt to seek union with God by great acts of piety, spiritual achievements, and religious accomplishments. While these efforts may not be intrinsically evil, they are detrimental to the spiritual life to the degree that they orient us towards self-sufficiency and a lack of dependence on the Lord. It is a pursuit of justice animated by a dangerous expectation of a return on a personal investment. In its worst expression, it is similar to treating God like a divine vending machine. I put in my quarter and wait to see if God gives me what I want. This attitude fails to make us humble and vulnerable to the will of the Lord and can even lead us away from the obedience His blessings require.

St. Thérèse makes the starting place of her self-offering her twofold awareness of her own inadequacy and the immense desire to give herself to God. Her awareness of inadequacy places her in a humble posture before the Lord. Her immense desire to console God's merciful love gives her confidence in what He can do in her life. She knows that only God could put such beautiful desires in her and because of His great goodness, He would never stir any desires except those that He intends to fulfill. In the desire to do something beautiful and purely for Him—

not despite her weakness but in the very midst of it—she finds reason to hope that she can make an offering of herself to Him.

St. Thérèse believed it was possible to be a living instrument of God's merciful love in the world, especially for those who most need the Lord's mercy, because He has made it so. In this mystery of His rejection and humiliation, the Lord has made space for us to share in His work of mercy. In this place our misery and the misery of Christ, His sorrows and our sorrows, coincide. St. Thérèse's oblation expresses her decision to stand with the Lord in this sacred place by bearing her own sorrows with faith and in the midst of them choosing to love just as He does.

She found through this solidarity the secret power of God was at work, accomplishing great wonders in the lives of those for whom she offered herself. It was as if her feeble efforts to surrender to the mercy of God made space for the Lord to do great things. In this way, she was convinced that her own love in the midst of difficult trials relieved Christ's misery in a very real, if imperfect, way. Her frail but repeated efforts allowed the Lord to do something beautiful. The love that moves her to offer herself to Merciful Love informs the spiritual wisdom that she has to share with the Church today.

The writings of this Doctor of the Church are filled with powerful insights into the inexhaustible mystery of Divine Mercy. Our reflections on St. Thérèse's words attempt to highlight her insights in a way that evokes the radical dedication to Merciful Love that she herself embraced. As a method for using this work in prayer, rather than reading several chapters in one sitting, we invite you to prayerfully read one of the selected passages from St. Thérèse's letters and then the reflection that we provide each day. After reading the passage and the reflection, underline phrases that strike you. Then, take at least a few minutes in silence to consider those truths. If the Lord pierces you to the heart through the wisdom of this great saint, take a moment to thank Him for that grace and for the gift of St. Thérèse. If your heart reaches a resolution about your way of life, consider writing it down so that you can go back to it throughout the day. Finally, to seal this time of prayer, we invite you to intentionally pray the Act of Oblation out loud at the end of each meditation as a way of preparing yourself for the mission of Divine Mercy that the Lord has entrusted to you for that day.

St. Thérèse of Lisieux wants to help you become a saint. Her letters were written to help those she loved realize this very purpose. Periodically throughout these thirty days, we encourage you to review your journal and think about how the Lord is speaking to you through this spiritual exercise. You might make some discoveries about God's will for you to bring to your spiritual director or to discuss with a spiritual friend. We hope that the entries you develop in your journal—whether your own insights or resolutions that you feel prompted to make—will become an important part of the story of *your* soul, an encouragement for yourself as well as those you love.

We believe that those who will allow St. Thérèse to teach them to make this oblation a part of their daily life of prayer will discover spiritual healing for themselves and for their loved ones. An indulgence was attached to this prayer as early as 1927. This means that whenever this oblation is offered with sincere devotion either for oneself or for someone who has gone before us in faith, Christ uses this prayer to help heal the wounds that sin has caused. The other conditions for the indulgence include going to Confession, receiving Communion, and praying for the intentions of the Holy Father. In addition to the wonderful grace offered through the Church, at the end of this thirty-day period of prayer, we hope that you will notice a deeper inclination to spend time with the Lord in silence and to extend the merciful love of God to others as part of your everyday life long after you have completed these reflections.

Day 1

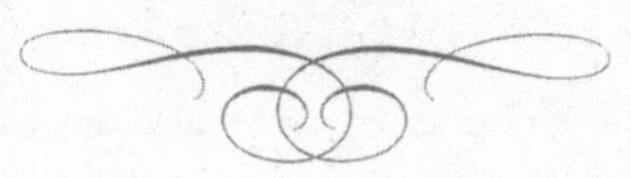

The Act of Oblation to Merciful Love
June 9, 1895

O My God! Blessed Trinity, I desire to Love you and make you Loved,
To work for the glory of the Holy Church
By saving souls on earth and by liberating those suffering in purgatory.
I desire to accomplish your will perfectly
And to reach the degree of glory that you have prepared for me in Your Kingdom.
I desire, in a word, to be Holy, but I feel my powerlessness
And I beg you, O my God! to be yourself my Holiness!

You loved me so much that you gave me your only Son
To be my Savior and my Spouse.
The infinite treasures of his merits are mine.
I offer them to you with gladness.
Look on me through the Face of Jesus and in his Heart burning with Love.

I offer you, too, all the merits of the saints in Heaven and on earth,
Their acts of Love, and those of the Holy Angels.

Finally, I offer You, O Blessed Trinity!
The Love and merits of the Blessed Virgin, my cherished Mother.
To her, I entrust my offering completely, imploring her to present it to you.

Her Divine Son, my Beloved Spouse, during his earthly life declared:
"Whatever you ask the Father in my name he will give to you!"
I am certain, therefore, that you will grant my desires; I know it, O my God!
The more you want to give, the more you make us desire.
I feel in my heart immense desires and
With confidence I ask you to come and take possession of my soul.

Ah! I cannot receive Holy Communion as often as I desire,
But, Lord, are you not all-powerful?
Remain in me as in a tabernacle and never separate yourself from your little victim.

I want to console you for the ingratitude of the wicked, and
I beg you to take my freedom to displease you away.
If through weakness I sometimes fall,
May your Divine Glance cleanse my soul immediately,
Consuming all my imperfections like fire that transforms everything into itself.

I thank You, O my God! for all the graces that you have granted me,
Especially the grace of making me pass through the crucible of suffering.
With joy I shall contemplate you on the Last Day
Carrying the scepter of your Cross.
Since you have chosen to give me a share in this very precious Cross,
I hope in heaven to resemble you
and to see shining in my glorified body the sacred stigmata of your Passion.

After earth's Exile, I hope to go and enjoy you in the Fatherland,
But I do not want to lay up merits for heaven.
I want to work for your Love Alone with the one purpose of pleasing you:

Day 1—The Act of Oblation to Merciful Love

To console your Sacred Heart, and to save souls who will love you forever.

In the evening of this life, I shall appear before you with empty hands.
Lord, I do not ask you to count my works.
All our justice is stained in your eyes.
I wish, then, to be clothed in your own Justice
And by your Love to receive you as my eternal possession.
No other Throne, no other Crown do I want but you, my Beloved!

Time is nothing in your eyes, and a single day is like a thousand years.
You can, then, in an instant prepare me to appear before You.

Finally, in order to live in an act of perfect Love,
I offer myself as a victim of holocaust to your Merciful Love.
I beg you to consume me incessantly.
Allow the waves of infinite tenderness shut up within you to overflow into my soul.
In this way, make me become a Martyr of your Love, O my God!

In the end, after it has prepared me to appear before you, may this martyrdom make me die.
May my soul take its flight without delay
Into the eternal embrace of your Merciful Love.

I want, O my Beloved, with each beat of my heart
to renew this offering to you an infinite number of times,
until the shadows are no more, and
I am able tell you of my Love in an Eternal Face to Face![1]

◆ ◆ ◆

St. Thérèse believes that God is ready to set our humanity on fire. Though we are guilty before the Face of God, the Father does not look

[1] Translated by Anthony Lilles. Original Source: *Story of A Soul,* translated by Fr. John Clarke, O.C.D., (Washington, DC: ICS Publications,1976), 276–278.

on us with anger, but gazes on us to contemplate His only begotten Son. He is no passive observer of human affairs. He stands ready to give everything to us for the asking—possession of all His merits, all His justice, all that is owed to Him for what He accomplished in His Humanity.

The dynamic vision of God presented by St. Thérèse cannot be overstated. The Trinity that St. Thérèse contemplates is involved in our plight, yet we have not caught on to the greatness of His purpose. We are helpless before the immensity of His love, but He is waiting for us, ready to act with power. Far from proposing a deity disappointed and distant, she cries out to the Almighty as the One surging with life and goodness towards us. She sees "shut up" in the Trinity "waves of infinite tenderness." She also sees that through union with Christ her own humble efforts to love become the key that unlocks torrents of tenderness. She roots this self-offering not on anything that she has achieved or accomplished for God. Instead, it is rooted in the power of prayer to obtain, or more precisely, "impetrate" or beg the Mercy of God. There are graces that God wants to give us, but He is waiting for us to ask with the right humility and devotion. Until we ask rightly, these graces are shut up in Him like a flood waiting to break forth from a dam.

The humility and the devotion that unlock the floodgates are not mental feats Thérèse manufactures on her own. The prayer that unleashes mercy is a gift of Christ, something that the Lord has given her possession of by faith. To express her assurance that God will hear her prayer, St. Thérèse quotes the words of Christ: "Whatsoever you ask the Father in my name he will give to you" (Jn 4:13). In her logic, the more frequently we rely on the Lord to offer ourselves in love, the more perfect our witness to God, and the more His love is unleashed. Yet she also knows that such love comes at a cost. One can only love at one's own expense—perfect love is offered "unto death." Thérèse is not confident in her own feeble efforts to this end. She is confident that the God who gives the desire to love this way will give all that is needed to do so. Thus, her offering is also a petition: "Be Thou my sanctity!"

The Act of Oblation that St. Thérèse offered and that we are preparing to make for ourselves orients us toward the immensity of God's saving love at work in the concrete moments of daily life and away from our own merits and accomplishments. This self-offering is at the heart of St. Thérèse's witness and it is offered out of love for the Lord who wishes to immerse our lives in His inexhaustible mercy. She invites her closest friends to make this sacrifice with her, and meditating on her letters from before and after this offering, we will be prepared to join them in doing something beautiful for God.

DAY 2

From Thérèse to Sr. Agnes of Jesus
March 18, 1888

OH! PAULINE, it is very true that a drop of gall must be mingled in all chalices; I find that trials help very much in detaching us from this earth. They make us look higher than this world. Here below, nothing can satisfy us. We cannot enjoy a little rest except in being ready to do God's will.

My little boat is having a lot of trouble reaching port. For a long time, I have seen the shore and I always find myself far off; but it is Jesus who is guiding my little boat, and I am sure that on the day when He wills it, it will be able to approach the port safely. Oh, Pauline, when Jesus will have placed me on the blessed shore of Carmel, I want to give myself totally to Him, I want to live no longer but for Him. Oh, no, I shall not fear His strikes, for, even in the most bitter sufferings, I always feel that it is His gentle hand that is striking. I really felt this at Rome at the very moment when I would have believed the earth could have given way beneath my steps.

I desire only one thing when I shall be in Carmel, and it is to suffer always for Jesus. Life passes so quickly that really it must be better to have a very beautiful crown and a little trouble than to have an ordinary one without any trouble. And then for a suffering borne with joy, when I think that during the whole of eternity I will love God better. Then in suffering we can save souls. Ah! Pauline, if at the moment of my death I could have a soul to offer to Jesus, how happy I would be; it would be a soul that would have been snatched from the fire of hell and would bless God for all eternity.

◆ ◆ ◆

Sr. Agnes is St. Thérèse's older sister. They share a very special bond, almost like a mother and daughter. St. Zélie Martin, their mother, died when Thérèse was very young and Pauline (which is Sr. Agnes' baptismal name) took over running the household and became an important maternal figure for her younger sister. Now, as St. Thérèse pursues her desire to become a Carmelite, she relies on the good counsel she receives from Sr. Agnes' spiritual maternity. In this letter, Thérèse confides how she interprets the difficult struggles that she is facing in trying to follow the will of the Lord.

Among the spiritual works of mercy, the Church lists patient endurance of hardship and praying for the living and the dead. This letter plunges into both of these expressions of God's love in us and points us to their inner connection. The witness of Thérèse invites us to view suffering not as a mere inconvenience to avoid or manage. In her letter, prayer and long-suffering converge in love. She proposes that the hardships we suffer can be offered to the Lord for the salvation of those whom He entrusts to us.

Several months before this letter to her sister, St. Thérèse had gone on a pilgrimage to Rome with her father, her sister Céline, and other pilgrims from her diocese. She was able to have an audience with Pope Leo XIII and, with a little prodding from Céline, boldly asked him to allow her to enter the Carmelite Monastery in Lisieux even though she was technically too young. She later realized that he was too elderly and enfeebled to understand her request. Yet she believed that she had been obedient to God in presenting herself. Her bishop did give the permission needed in the weeks that followed her trip to Rome. Even still, her desire to enter Carmel was not realized instantly. After a couple months of patient waiting, she begins to see that her "trouble reaching port" is "a drop of gall." God is offering her a chalice just like the chalice Christ accepted in Gethsemane. Her disappointment was crucifying, and like a drop of gall detaching her, helped to fix her gaze on those things that are from above. For Thérèse, the goal is not to avoid suffering or even to manage this difficulty until at last she is able to live her Carmelite vocation. The goal is to love. And in this life, love is revealed through the suffering we endure for it. Her ultimate goal is to suffer with Christ Jesus—to renounce herself, pick up her cross, and follow Him.

In this life, things often fail to work out the way we want. If we allow disappointment to pull us down into bitterness or anxiety, our lives risk a certain banality.

St. Thérèse is not simply resigned about her situation. She has made a decision to bear it with joy. Thérèse is not pretending to be elated or making sure that others are not aware of her disappointment; nor does she try to work herself into a positive emotional state. Instead, she seeks in her disappointment the mysterious way that God is at work in the situation. More than resignation, seeking out His will in this difficult ambiguity allows her to surrender to His loving work. Suffering with this kind of joy is a "beautiful crown."

When our plans run amiss, it takes faith to believe that Divine Providence is still at work. Assenting to this does not completely diminish the hardship, but it does allow us to choose to accept what God is doing in both the desires of our hearts and the circumstances that befall us. With hope, we keep the true goal in mind and deepen our dedication to the designs of God's heart.

When we choose to live by faith in difficult circumstances rather than succumbing to the emotions of the moment, suffering can become an offering on behalf of the spiritual needs of our brothers and sisters.

When this happens, we realize, like Thérèse, the convergence of long-suffering and prayer, two works of mercy so intimately connected.

DAY 3

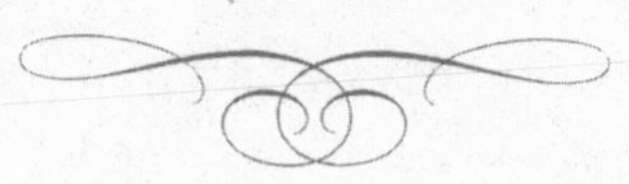

From Thérèse to Céline
January 25, 1889

CÉLINE . . . JESUS must love you with a special love to be trying you in this way. Do you know that I am almost jealous of you? To those who love more He gives *more*, and to those who love less He gives less! . . .

But you don't feel your love for Your Spouse. You would like your heart to be a flame that rises up to Him without the lightest smoke. Don't forget that the smoke that surrounds you is only for yourself in order to remove you from the sight of your love for Jesus, while the flame is only for Him. At last, then He has this love entirely, for if He were to show it to us just a little bit, swiftly self-love would come like a fatal wind which extinguishes everything! . . .

You give me the impression, at this moment, of a person who is surrounded by immense riches . . . the sight of them is lost over the horizon. . . . This person wants to turn her back because, she says, too many riches embarrass her, she does not know what to do with them; it is better to lose them, or that *another* take them! . . . That other will not come, for these riches are prepared for the fiancée of Jesus . . . and for her alone! . . . God would turn the world upside down to find suffering in order to give it to a soul upon whom His DIVINE *glance* has rested with an indescribable love! . . .

The things of the earth . . . what do they mean to us? . . . Should this be our homeland, this *slime*, so unworthy of an immortal soul . . . and what does it matter that cowardly men *harvest* the mustiness that grows on this slime? The more our heart is in heaven the less we feel these *pinpricks*. . . .

But believe that this is a *grace* and a *great grace* to feel these pinpricks, for, then, our life is a *martyrdom*, and one day Jesus will give us the palm. To suffer and to be *despised*! . . . what *bitterness* but what glory.

◆ ◆ ◆

St. Thérèse's reflections on suffering as "immense riches" and humiliation as a "pinprick" present us with unconventional judgments. They seem to oppose the basic tenets of earthly happiness and jar our sensibilities. It would be easy to reduce her musings to a vaguely religious but unhealthy attitude not in touch with the real world. Yet, what she is trying to express to her sister Céline in this letter is a real word of encouragement.

The foundation for her judgments is the Gospel of Christ. In particular, Jesus' Sermon on the Mount holds up this same paradox of suffering and blessedness. Christ declares that the poor, the sorrowing, the meek, those who thirst for justice, the pure of heart, those who work for peace, and those persecuted for righteousness' sake are all are blessed and great in the kingdom of heaven. This order of things is not part of our tangible experience. It is something mysterious and spiritual that we cleave to by faith. It is within this Gospel context that we must situate her message to Céline. This letter represents a word of hope to someone whom St. Thérèse believes the mysterious blessedness of the Gospel fully applies.

From this perspective, suffering, humiliation, hardships, and difficulties are not obstacles to happiness. They are God-given opportunities waiting for our generous response. God permits those He loves to suffer only because He has transformed human misery by entering into it and sharing it with us. When we seek Him in the midst of trial, He communicates spiritual riches that we could not have received in any other way. Through the Passion of Christ, human suffering has become a medium for divine blessing.

Like Thérèse, Céline was also undergoing a trial in her vocation. Even as they sought to enter Carmel, St. Louis Martin, their father, had declined under the weight of mental illness. The girls were accused of being more concerned with becoming nuns than they were with taking care of their widowed father. It was a double trial. Thérèse and her sisters experienced not only the stress of a surviving parent's poor health, but also faced the humiliation of gossip and detraction.

Such was the mysterious blessing of persecution and sorrow for their father, together with their patient endurance concerning the desires of their hearts. Thérèse's basic message is that the suffering and humiliation were great because God loved Céline with a very uncommon love. Rather than be overwhelmed by the Lord's generosity, Thérèse counseled her to be grateful, to respond with an excess of love for the love that she was receiving. This example provides us with a new perspective when we are misunderstood and when we face difficult circumstances over which we have little control. More than merely resisting the temptation to lose heart or indulge in some form of self-pity, Thérèse's judgment about suffering and humiliation beckons us to courage and gratitude. Rather than identifying as victims of circumstance, she helps us find dignity in the way the Lord has chosen to love us.

DAY 4

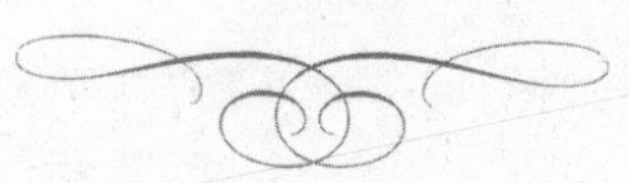

From Thérèse to Céline
April 4, 1889

JESUS! . . .

Dear Little Céline,

Your letter gave great sadness to my soul! Poor little Papa! . . . No, the thoughts of Jesus are not our thoughts, and His ways are not our ways. . . .

He is offering us a chalice as bitter as our feeble nature can bear! . . . Let us not withdraw our lips from this chalice prepared by the hand of Jesus. . . .

Let us see life as it really is. . . . It is a moment between two *eternities*. . . . Let us suffer in *peace*! . . .

I admit that this word peace seemed a little strong to me, but the other day, when reflecting on it, I found the secret of suffering in peace. . . . The one who says *peace* is not saying joy, or at least, *felt* joy. . . . To suffer in peace is enough to will all that Jesus wills. . . . To be the spouse of Jesus we *must* resemble Jesus, and Jesus is all bloody, he is crowned with thorns! . . .

"A thousand years in your eyes, Lord, are as yesterday, which has *passed*"! . . .

"On the banks of the river of Babylon, we sat and wept when we remembered Sion. . . . We hung up our harps on the willows in the fields. . . . Those who led us into captivity said to us: 'Sing for us one of the pleasant songs from Sion.' How could we sing the song of the Lord in a foreign land!" . . .

No, let us not sing the canticles of heaven to creatures. . . . But, like Cecelia, let us sing a melodious canticle in our heart to our Beloved! . . .

The canticle of suffering united to His sufferings is what delights His Heart the most! . . .

Jesus is on fire with love for us . . . look at His adorable Face! . . . Look at His eyes lifeless and lowered! Look at His wounds. . . . Look at Jesus in His Face . . . . There you will see how He loves us.

◆ ◆ ◆

Like her little sister, Céline also wanted to enter Carmel. With maternal affection, she put St. Thérèse's vocation ahead of her own and spiritually accompanied Thérèse through all the trials she endured in order to enter Carmel early. Now, Céline was having to deal with a very difficult situation. This letter is offered to encourage Céline not only in her vocation but also her faith.

Their father, Louis Martin, suffered from several strokes and cerebral arteriosclerosis, a hardening of the arteries of the brain. The condition caused hallucinations, anxiety, and forgetfulness. Although he was a loving father and would eventually be canonized a saint, he suffered from bouts of moodiness and irritation. After St. Thérèse entered Carmel, Céline stayed behind to care for him. Not always capable of distinguishing between reality and fantasy, Louis soon walked off without a word. With the help of her uncle, Céline eventually found him, but realized that her father would need special care for the rest of his life. He was committed to a mental hospital, where he made some progress for a time. Then, when doctors decided to discontinue his medications, his condition worsened. Since his physiological condition was not understood, his mental breakdown was attributed by many to the stress of having been abandoned by his daughters.

Even before all this unfolded, Céline's vocation was put to the test. On top of the stress of attempting to care for her ailing father, a young man had proposed to her. The life she had imagined for herself was now turned upside down. The decision to decline this generous offer could not have been easily made. The marriage would have allowed her to attend to her father. It might also have allayed some of the gossip about the family. With his worsened state, it would have been normal for her to question her earlier decision. But, instead of relying on a natural answer to her family's plight, Céline had chosen to give herself to God. Her resolve not only about her vocation but about how to live her faith was under fire. In the face of these doubts, Thérèse gently proposes a supernatural way forward.

To offer her counsel, Thérèse places herself in solidarity with Céline. She spiritually joins herself to Céline's humiliation and makes it something that they endure together with and for their saintly father. This particular suffering is a chalice, like the chalice that Christ received in the Garden of Gethsemane. By the mystery of their union with Christ, the two of them will spiritually accompany their father in the agony and humiliation of mental illness, a mysterious kind of crucifixion.

In order to deepen their solidarity in love and prayer, St. Thérèse proposes her secret to suffering in peace. Some believe that the secret of suffering in peace is to pretend to be joyful. This is not St. Thérèse's counsel. She does not ask Céline to act as if she felt joyful about their father's illness or about their humiliations. Instead, Thérèse implies there is another kind of joy besides the kind that is felt. Instead of trying to expound on this spiritual joy, she draws Céline's attention to a related fruit of the spirit: peace. The peace that comes from God is not based on feelings or psychic states. The Holy Spirit produces spiritual fruits in the very depths of our being and they transform the way we deal with sorrow. Sorrow can weigh upon our existence and emotionally paralyze us. But if we give the Holy Spirit space to act in us, He infuses our sorrow with confidence in the love of the Lord. A desire to do something that delights the Lord is born in the heart as it becomes more confident in His love. Christ's love is what helps us find a mysterious joy and peace in the midst of difficult trials.

What gives the Holy Spirit this room to act in us? Mental prayer. It is an important effort of the Christian life. Mental prayer searches the face of Christ, not only with one's imagination, but with one's real awareness by faith of His presence and His saving mysteries. The Holy Face of Christ helped St. Thérèse keep the eyes of her heart fixed on the Lord. And this way, His will for her became the ground on which she was able to stand firm. If we do not spend time seeking out the Lord "on fire with love for us," we will not find the firm ground on which to live our lives in peace. Rather, through silent reflection on His loving presence, His Holy Face can reveal the eternity that frames this present moment and alleviate the hardships and trials we must endure.

Faith re-orients our perspective on the difficult moments of life. These moments are not absolute. They pass. They are part of the transition from one eternity to the next. God who is eternal has called us into eternal life, and through the suffering of Christ is sanctifying this present moment, setting it aside so that it can be one more moment that brings us closer to Him.

St. Teresa of Ávila, the Carmelite reformer and spiritual mother of St. Thérèse, wrote in her breviary, "All things are passing, God never changes." Difficult times come and go, but God remains. God created us in peace and He invites us into the peace of His life and love. For us to freely move from eternity to eternity in the present moment, we must go by the same peace from which we came and toward which we are ordered: the peace of the Lord. To lose our peace by allowing ourselves to be stirred up by contention or anxiety will not help us make progress from one eternity to the next. The only path of peace is a pathway of greater and greater union with the will of God.

What does St. Thérèse mean when she invites Céline to will what Jesus wills? She is offering a challenge to rise above trials and hardships, especially when they involve those whom one loves in a particular way. It is a call to patiently endure all difficulties out of love, to delight His Heart. As we live this moment between two eternities, our likeness—and our nearness—to the crucified and humiliated Christ increases.

DAY 5

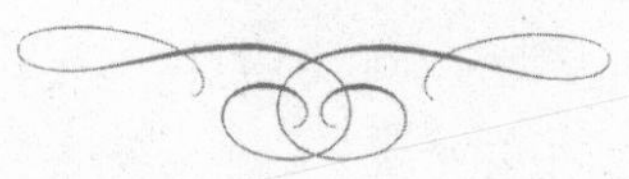

From Thérèse to Marie Guérin
May 30, 1889

My dear little Sister,

You did well to write to me, and I understand *everything . . . everything, everything, everything!* . . .

You haven't committed the *shadow of any evil*; I know what these kinds of temptations are so well that I can assure you of this without any fear, and, besides, Jesus tells me this in the depths of my heart . . . . We must despise temptations and pay no attention whatsoever to them.

Should I tell you something that has given me *much* sorrow? . . .

It is that my little Marie has given up her Communions . . . on the feast of the Ascension and on the last day of Mary's month! . . . Oh! What sorrow this has caused Jesus! . . .

The devil has to be very clever to mislead a soul in this way! . . . But don't you know, my dear, that this is the only goal of his desires? The evil one knows well that he can't make a soul that wants to belong totally to Jesus commit a sin, so he tries to make the soul believe it has. It is already much for him to put disturbance in this soul, but to satisfy his rage something else is needed; he wants to deprive Jesus of a loved tabernacle, and, not being able to enter his sanctuary, he wants, at least, that it remain *empty* and without any Master! . . . Alas, what will become of this poor heart? . . . When the devil has succeeded in drawing the soul away from Holy Communion, he *has won everything* . . . . And Jesus weeps! . . .

Oh, my darling, think, then, that Jesus is there in the Tabernacle expressly for *you*, for *you alone*; He is burning with the desire to enter your heart . . . so don't listen to the devil, mock him, and go without any fear to receive Jesus in peace and love! . . .

However, I hear you saying to me: "Thérèse is saying this because she doesn't know . . . she doesn't know I really do it on purpose . . . it pleases me . . . and so I cannot receive Communion since I believe I would be committing a sacrilege, etc., etc., ..." Yes, your poor little Thérèse does know; I tell you that she understands it *all*, and she assures you that you can go without any fear to receive your only true Friend . . . . She, too, has passed through the *martyrdom* of scruples, but Jesus has given her the grace to receive Communion just the same, even when she believed that she had committed *great sins* . . . . And so I assure you that she knew this was the sole means of ridding herself of the devil, for when he sees that he is losing this time, he leaves you in peace! . . .

No, it is IMPOSSIBLE that a heart "which rests only at the sight of the Tabernacle" offend Jesus to the point of not being able to receive Him; what offends Him and what wounds His Heart is the lack of confidence! . . .

Your heart is made to love Jesus, to love Him passionately; pray so that the *beautiful years of your life* may not pass by in chimerical fears.

We have only the short moments of our life to love Jesus, and the devil knows this well, and so he tries to consume our life in useless works. . . .

Dear little sister, *receive Communion often*, very often. . . . That is the *only remedy* if you want to be healed, and Jesus hasn't placed this attraction in your soul for nothing. (I believe that He would be pleased if you could receive the two Communions you missed, for, then, the devil's victory would be less great since he would not have succeeded in separating Jesus from your heart.) Have no fear of loving the Blessed Virgin *too much*, you will *never* love her enough, and Jesus will be pleased since the Blessed Virgin is His Mother.

Adieu, little sister; pardon my scribbling which I can't even read over since I don't have the time. Kiss all my dear ones for me.

◆ ◆ ◆

Marie Guérin is a cousin to St. Thérèse and just a few years older than her. After St. Zélie Martin died, the family eventually moved to Lisieux to be closer to their cousins and Thérèse began attending school with Marie. Now teenagers, they enjoyed a close relationship throughout their childhood. Like Thérèse, Marie is also called to enter Carmel. But unlike Thérèse, it will take several more years for her to be ready to enter.

In the emphatic beginning of this letter, Thérèse attempts to reassure her cousin that she understands her spiritual suffering. The reason that she repeats that she understands "everything, everything, everything!" is that only a few years before, Thérèse herself had experienced the depressing and overwhelming fear that scrupulosity can sometimes cause. Marie is suffering from this same spiritual disease which leaves one feeling deeply ashamed, alienated, and without hope. The only medicine that can cure this illness of soul is a new openness to the love of God. Mental prayer and frequent reception of Holy Communion are the normal means that God uses to produce this openness. However, the problem with scrupulosity is that the person afflicted does not believe that they are worthy to receive Communion. As long as they stay focused on their own unworthiness rather than the mercy of God, they succeed in cutting themselves off from the healing grace of the Eucharist and the contemplation that flows from it.

This letter has become one of the greatest spiritual contributions to the teaching and practice of the Church because it passionately proposes the counsel to receive Holy Communion often. After the death of St. Thérèse, Pope St. Pius X read this letter and became convinced that the process for her canonization needed to move forward. He would, in fact, advocate for the frequent reception of Holy Communion and even lowered the age for First Communion to help encourage this. He did so to combat, with St. Thérèse, a false sense of unworthiness that prevented many from receiving the sacrament when they most needed it.

◆ ◆ ◆

During St. Thérèse's lifetime, receiving daily Communion was an uncommon practice. A constricted fearfulness, known as Jansenism, discouraged the frequent reception of Communion. In the heresy of Jansenism, fear of divine punishment can overshadow confidence in Divine Mercy. The opposite spiritual error would be presumption, by which one would seek to selfishly grasp the divine mysteries with little reverence for God or concern for His ways. St. Thérèse counsels her cousin to avoid the extremes of both fearfulness and presumption by focusing her attention on the purpose of God's love in Holy Communion. This lack of confidence in Christ's love contributes to the unhealthy scrupulosity that Thérèse recognized as afflicting Marie. Her counsel here is especially applicable for souls so paralyzed by their failures that they forget that God's love, not their shortcomings, is the determining factor in the life of faith.

At the time, very few Catholics, no matter how devout, felt worthy to receive Holy Communion. Even today, the temptation to feel unworthy for Holy Communion can be a serious trial. Satan loves to torment, isolate, and cut us off from the means of grace. This is why, in our struggle against sin, it is important to discuss with a spiritual director and a confessor the conditions under which one should not receive Holy Communion. Unless it is clear that we sinned with full knowledge and freedom in an area involving grave matter, we should normally avail ourselves of Holy Communion as often as possible. We must not allow evil spiritual forces to separate us from the healing love of God offered in the sacraments, especially the Eucharist.

Thérèse's message is especially useful for those souls who want to please God and who normally live a life worthy of their great calling and yet have ongoing struggles because of bad habits from the past or because they are so ashamed of their sins that they forget the power of God's mercy. Behind this lack of confidence in the mercy of God is a certain pride that can only be overcome by persevering in prayer and making every effort to go to Communion as frequently as possible—preferably daily. Anyone who, in a moment of weakness, backslides or, because of repeated failures, feels too ashamed to appeal to the mercy of God should know that He is never tired of forgiving us.

Going to Mass and receiving Holy Communion allows God to heal those sins that we commit in the face of diminished personal freedom. As we struggle to be faithful in our weakness and inadequacy, frequent reception of the sacraments is a necessary source of spiritual healing and strength. It is for these reasons that St. Thérèse rightly counters the poor spiritual teaching of her day. In this, she helps her cousin find a more sure path to intimacy with the Lord.

In this case, Marie Guerrin, who otherwise lives a very devout life, decided not to receive Communion because she was ashamed of her failure. A scrupulous soul finds it difficult to trust anyone because they are certain that no one understands their sin. St. Thérèse does, however, because she too had faced scrupulosity earlier in life. Thérèse knows the demonic logic that caused Marie to lose her confidence in God's merciful love. Her own experience allows her to anticipate Marie's objections ("She doesn't know I really do it on purpose").

Since the time of St. Antony the Great, the Church has recognized demonic temptation as an alienating influence. Satan is a seducer. Satanic powers constantly attempt to accuse and confuse the faithful until they feel completely disconnected from God and from anyone who might offer them a word of hope. The first and most important step to resisting these kinds of efforts is to identify them for what they are. This is why St. Thérèse is so forceful and clear about the source of Marie's internal torment. She does not counsel Marie to take sin lightly, but she tries to help her recognize the influence of evil spirits. Unlike diabolical influences, the Holy Spirit convinces us of sin to move us towards repentance and reconciliation. The Spirit of Love never oppresses or discourages, but instead directs us to spiritual freedom. In order to make progress in our love for the Lord, Thérèse is encouraging us to distinguish the conviction of the Holy Spirit from the alienating accusations of the Evil One. Our faith requires that we renounce all evil lies—especially those lies which suggest that we are too unworthy to approach the Lord with faith.

Thérèse believes in frequent Communion as a source of healing for the sins we commit every day. Her conviction about the healing power of daily Communion is in alignment with the teaching of St. Thomas Aquinas, who explains how participating at Mass actually forgives venial sins. These kinds of sins are not a rejection of God or His will, as is the case with mortal or deadly sins. Instead, these kinds of sins involve a lack of love. It is helpful to confess these as often as possible, but venial sins do not have to be confessed before receiving Communion. Instead, whenever we participate at Mass with devotion and receive Communion with faith in the Lord's Real Presence, this act of love fills us with the grace that heals and perfects our love.

Thérèse is not recommending that Marie be casual or presumptuous, but that she be confident in God's immense love for her. Thérèse knows that Marie has not acted deliberately against God's will. Her wise counsel goes beyond simply discerning the tactics of the evil one. Not only must we identify and renounce his lies, we must reject his lies *and* act against his counsels. If he prompts us not to go to Communion or to postpone going to confession, we should renew our efforts to return to the sacraments as soon as possible.

Every Christian needs someone to help them in the discernment of spirits. We need the wise counsel of those who know us and can help us see our lives in relation to God's particular love for us. If evil spirits try to alienate us from one another, it is because they know that God uses our brothers and sisters to help us discover helpful truths. In these kinds of situations, a good confessor and a good spiritual director are both very important.

Contemplative prayer has a special role to play in our spiritual battles. If the Lord passionately desires to enter into Marie's heart, it means that He has already taken up her side and stands with her against the "accuser of the brethren" (Rev 12:10). The Eucharistic presence of Jesus that Marie is encouraged to rediscover in prayer is not passive or remote, but dynamic and close at hand. To engage in contemplative prayer is to learn how much the Lord desires intimacy with us. The loving awareness that Thérèse is inviting Marie to make her own is the very contemplation of God that informs her Oblation to Merciful Love:

> I am certain, then, that You will grant my desires; I know, O my God! that the more You want to give, the more You make us desire. I feel in my heart immense desires and it is with confidence I ask You to come and take possession of my soul. Ah! I cannot receive Holy Communion as often as I desire, but, Lord, are You not all-powerful? Remain in me as in a tabernacle and never separate Yourself from Your little victim.

To offer oneself as a victim of Merciful Love means devoting oneself to attending Mass and receiving Communion as often as possible. As we receive Holy Communion with a proper disposition and greater frequency and devotion, we avail ourselves of the same certainty and "immense desires" that St. Thérèse puts at the heart of her self-offering. This confidence in the power of the Lord and in His generosity to those whom He loves allows us to give ourselves to Him more completely and with greater freedom—even to the point that nothing can diminish our awareness of His loving presence by faith.

DAY 6

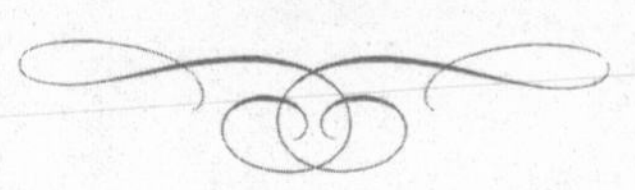

From Thérèse to Sr. Agnes of Jesus
August 1889

Little Belloni of Jesus, pray for the poor little grain of sand, that the grain of sand be always in its place, that is to say, under the feet of all, that no one may think of it, that its existence be, so to speak, *unknown*. The grain of sand does not desire to be *humbled*; this is still too glorious since one would be obliged to be occupied with it. It desires one thing, to be FORGOTTEN, counted for *nothing*! . . . But it desires to be *seen* by *Jesus*. If the eyes of creatures cannot be lowered to look at it, may, at least, the blood-stained Face of Jesus be turned towards it. . . . It desires only one look, one look! . . .

If it were possible for a grain of sand to console Jesus, to wipe away His tears, there really is such a grain that would like to do it. . . .

May Jesus take the poor grain of sand and hide it in His adorable Face. . . . There, the poor atom will no longer have anything to fear, it will be sure of *no longer sinning*!

The grain of sand wants at all costs to save souls. . . . Jesus must grant it this grace. Little Veronica, ask this grace from the *luminous* face of Jesus! . . . Yes, the Face of Jesus is *luminous*, but if in the midst of wounds and tears it is already so beautiful, what will it be, then, when we shall see it in heaven? Oh, heaven . . . heaven. Yes, to see one day the

Face of Jesus, to contemplate eternally the marvelous beauty of Jesus, the poor grain of sand desires to be despised on earth! . . .

Dear lamb, beg Jesus that His grain of sand hurry to save many souls in a short time in order to take its flight promptly towards *His dear Face*! . . .

I am suffering! . . . But the hope of the homeland gives me courage, soon we shall be in heaven! . . . In heaven, there will no longer be day or night, but the Face of Jesus will make an incomparable light shine! . . .

◆ ◆ ◆

Devotion to the Holy Face of the Lord informs the spiritual mission of St. Thérèse. Her full name is Thérèse of the Child Jesus and of the Holy Face. The Holy Face is a devotion to the image of Christ's face left on the veil of Veronica, who wiped His face on the way to Calvary. This devotion explores the humanity of Christ who suffered for us. It places one's whole life in relation to the suffering revealed in the face of Christ. While this devotion invites us to imagine what the face of the Lord looked like during His Passion, in this letter St. Thérèse's thoughts are not on anything her imagination conceives about Christ. Instead, she is intently focused on the fact that she hopes Christ sees her and even more, that in seeing her, He is somehow consoled by what He sees.

◆ ◆ ◆

Viewing oneself as a grain of sand might not be constructive if it is erroneously interpreted in terms of the modern conception of low self-esteem. Thérèse wants to be seen by Jesus but forgotten by everyone else. She wants to be anonymous to the world so that she might more fully belong to Him. Today, we live with such a desire to be noticed and seen by others, many might find the desires expressed by St. Thérèse to be psychologically unhealthy. At the same time, it could be argued that excessive concern with what others think can also be stifling. In order to offer ourselves as living sacrifices to Divine Mercy, we need freedom from the desire to protect and promote our reputations.

As long as we are caught up in self-promotion, we are distracted from the presence of Christ in the world around us. Christ Crucified identified with the rejected, the lowly, and the humble. He declared the poor and meek to be blessed. He told His disciples that unless they deny themselves, pick up their crosses, and follow Him, they could not be His disciples. By calling herself a grain of sand and desiring that she be "unknown," St. Thérèse is choosing not to seek the approval and recognition of others. She is choosing instead to identify with Christ who became sin and permitted Himself to be despised for her sake. In *Ascent to Mount Carmel*, St. John of the Cross writes that the most sure way to imitate Christ is to prefer to be misunderstood and despised by others, rather than loved and honored. This does not mean that love and honor are not good. It means simply that we are not free to follow Christ as long as we prefer the love and honor of others more than His. St. John of the Cross knows that freedom from these distractions is required for our love of God to be made perfect. In this letter, St. Thérèse is appropriating the spirit of this counsel in her life.

It is believed that in addition to the gossip damaging the reputation of Thérèse's whole family both inside and outside of the convent, St. Thérèse herself may have been facing a new bout of scruples when she penned this letter. It is noteworthy that rather than explore her unworthiness, she focuses on her seeming insignificance before others, her desire that Christ might recognize her with His Holy Face. She longs to see His Face and the look of love that is there through the blood that He shed for her. This longing is carrying her through a difficult trial. St. Thérèse has chosen to believe in the love of Christ more than her own wretchedness, and she believes that His saving look is greater than her failure. This conviction finds its way into the Act of Oblation: "If through weakness I sometimes fall, may Your Divine Glance cleanse my soul immediately, consuming all my imperfections like the fire that transforms everything into itself."

The gaze of Christ cleanses us. This is what St Thérèse contemplates in the Holy Face. Her prayer goes beyond intuition and insight into Christ's love. It is an encounter with that love, a transformative meeting that anticipates a face-to-face with the Lord in heaven. Christian contemplation is not an accomplishment of the intellect or the imagination. It is not a state of consciousness that one achieves. Christian contemplation allows one to be vulnerable enough to be seen by Christ and to fully take in this powerful moment of recognition and love. To allow oneself to be seen by the One who was crucified for our sake is a purifying moment that is worth losing everything else in life to attain.

Day 7

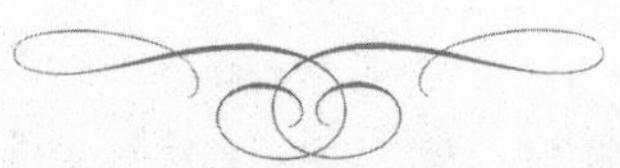

From Thérèse to Marie Guérin
July 27, 1890

My dear little Marie,

Thank God for all the graces He is giving you, and don't be so *ungrateful* as to not acknowledge them. You gave me the impression of a little country girl to whom a powerful king should come and ask her to marry him, and she would not dare to accept under the pretext that she is not rich enough and schooled enough in the ways of the court, without realizing that her royal fiancé is aware of her poverty and weakness much better than she is herself. . . . Marie, if you are nothing, you must not forget that Jesus is *All*, so you must lose your little nothingness in His *infinite All* and think only of his uniquely loveable *All*. . . . neither ought you desire to see the fruit gathered from your efforts, for Jesus is pleased to keep for Himself alone these little nothings that console Him . . . . You are mistaken, my darling, if you believe that your little Thérèse walks always with fervor on the road of virtue. She is weak and very weak, and every day she has a new experience of this weakness, but, Marie, Jesus is pleased to teach her, as He did St. Paul, the science of rejoicing in her infirmities. This is a great grace, and I beg Jesus to teach it to you, for peace and quiet of heart are to be found there only. When we see ourselves as so miserable, then we no longer wish to consider ourselves, and we look only on the unique Beloved! . . .

Dear little Marie, as for myself, I know no other means of reaching perfection but (love). . . . Love, how well our heart is made for that! . . . Sometimes, I seek for another word to express love, but on this earth of exile words are powerless to express all the soul's vibrations, so we have to keep to this one word: (love!). . . .

But upon whom will our poor heart hungry for love bestow it? . . . Ah, who will be big enough for this . . . will a human person be able to understand it . . . and, above all, will he know how to return it? Marie, there is only one Being who can understand the profundity of this word: Love! . . . It is only our Jesus who knows how to return infinitely more than we give Him . . . .

Marie of the Blessed Sacrament! . . . Your name speaks your mission. . . . Console Jesus, make Him *loved* by souls. . . . Jesus is sick, and we must state that the sickness of love is healed only through love! . . . Marie, really give your whole heart to Jesus, He is thirsty for it, He is hungry for it. Your heart, this is what He longs for, even to the point that to have it for Himself He consents to lodge under a dirty and hidden nook! . . . Ah! How not to love a Friend who reduces Himself to such extreme indigence, and how does one dare speak of one's poverty when Jesus makes Himself like His fiancée. . . . He was rich and He made Himself poor in order to unite His poverty to the poverty of Marie of the Blessed Sacrament. . . . What a mystery of love! . . .

◆ ◆ ◆

The spiritual life is often hampered by a lack of gratitude. We have been so richly blessed, but instead of lifting up our minds to the Lord's goodness, we wallow in self-pity or false humility. God has offered us everything and is waiting for our reply. Instead of lifting our hearts to Him, we beat ourselves up for our inadequacies. Some might think this is the opposite of pride, an act of humility. But that is not the case. Accusing ourselves of sin only has value to the degree that it leads us to conversion of heart and a deeper faith in the mercy of God. When we accuse ourselves for any other reason, we merely bury the graces given to us in self-torment.

Think about the Lord's parable of the talents. The only servant who was punished was the one who buried what was entrusted to him. When his master asked this servant why he acted in this way, it is clear that the servant was afraid of punishment. There is a pride hidden in this fear. Instead of accepting the responsibility entrusted to him by the master, the servant decided not to serve because he was afraid of failure. Self-accusation can lead to fear of failure, which keeps us from serving God. Because the servant did not act out of his master's confidence in him, but instead saw himself as the potential object of punishment, he failed to be industrious. Here, false humility is any rejection of what the Father sees. It is in denial of the loving gaze of the Father that pride decides "I will not serve," even when it masks itself in fear of punishment. This means that, if we are not careful, spiritual pride can be at work in us whenever we wallow in our failures.

Love alone overcomes fear and pride. St. Thérèse is helping Marie of the Trinity through her struggle by offering a new perspective that comes from turning our eyes from our own unworthiness and allowing ourselves to be astonished that He who knows us better than we know ourselves has come to rescue us. He is undaunted by our shame and failure, and the secret to living in His mercy is to allow His faithfulness to pierce us to the heart.

The nothingness we must lose is our own self-preoccupation. The more we indulge in thoughts about ourselves—or what should happen to us, or what we are owed or not owed, what we deserve or do not deserve—the farther our thoughts are taking us from God. He is what *is*—ultimate truth. He is always at work in surprising ways and no matter how much we know about Him, we only make ourselves aware of how He exceeds our powers to know.

St. Thérèse proposes that this unfathomable divine mystery is uniquely loveable and likens it to a Bridegroom-King who has come to claim his Bride. She is not proposing that the love He is owed is merely a general and vague religious feeling. He evokes a unique love; a love unique to each person and that uniquely belongs to Him. This love also makes an absolute claim: it is infinite and All in such a way that all else must be regarded as both limited and secondary. This includes our own inadequacies and feelings of unworthiness. Our inability to be as devout as we ought is not the ultimate truth about our lives. Our personal failures do not ultimately define us in the face of God's love. Rather it is the infinite and uniquely loveable All of God who is the reference point and defining center of our own personal existence. To think about this aligns our minds with what actually is the case. Not to think about this and to torment ourselves about our weaknesses is to cleave to emptiness.

We make ourselves vulnerable to the heart-piercing love of God by choosing to think about the fullness of His love and blessings, even when they seem hidden in the difficult circumstances of the moment. God's infinite and uniquely loveable All—and the truth that He is present and at work—is the ultimate reality in each situation. To penetrate this mystery requires that we discipline our thoughts and direct our attention to the truth before us. Self-preoccupation imprisons us, but we find freedom through cultivating an awareness of God's presence by faith.

Besides cleaving to the presence of God and allowing ourselves to be pierced by the love of the One who has come for us, St. Thérèse also speaks of the "science" of "rejoicing in her infirmities." Thérèse knows of no other pathway to holiness than that which this particular kind of knowledge provides. Feelings of fervor come and go. A sense of divine approval or a consoling awareness of His presence usually does not last. Yet, if we learn to rejoice in the midst of difficulties, we avail ourselves of hidden and unfamiliar graces we would otherwise never know. These are graces that deepen our love for God even to the point that we ache for love of Him.

Thérèse invites her reader to the most profound kind of union with the Lord that can be known in this life. She contemplates Jesus sick with love. To console Jesus is a matter of being present to Him and attending to the priorities in His heart. As we ponder this mystery and allow its gravity to pull at our hearts, a beautiful desire is evoked in the depths of our spirits. It is a movement of compassion for God. When we intentionally set them before the ardent longing of Christ to relieve our plight that burns in Him, our own hearts can be set on fire. And then a new kind of selflessness is born in us. We soon find ourselves offering our own sufferings to the Lord with love and asking Him to join these to Himself. Through His mysterious power at work in us, He is able to use this act of love to unleash His tenderness in a particular moment of our lives, in a way that relieves the suffering of those whom He has entrusted to us. Somehow, when we deny ourselves and surrender to the designs of His Heart, we have made space for the Lord to affirm the dignity of our neighbor and to give them a sense that they are not alone.

This movement to console the Heart of Jesus and to help make Him loved by others is not limited to isolated instances. As our love is perfected, one moment of mercy leads to another moment. We discover that we ache for love all the more as this proceeds. The more we ache for love we also discover that we are able to more deeply love. As Thérèse observes, "The sickness of love is only healed through love."

DAY 8

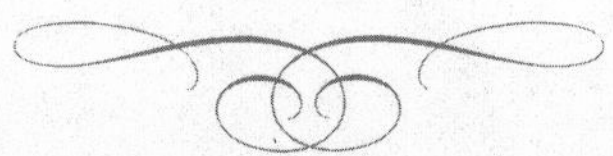

From Thérèse to Sr. Agnes of Jesus
August 30, 1890

If you only knew what your letter says to my soul! . . .

But the little hermit must tell you of the itinerary of her trip and here it is. Before she left, her Fiancé seemed to ask her in what country she desired to travel, what route she desired to follow, etc., etc. . . . The little fiancée answered that she had but one desire, that of being taken to the summit of the *mountain of Love*. To reach it many routes were offered to her, and there were so many perfect ones that she saw she was incapable of choosing. There she said to her divine guide: "You know where I want to go, You know *for whom* I want to climb the mountain, for whom I want to reach the goal. You know the one whom I love and the one whom I want to please solely; it is for Him alone that I am undertaking this journey. Lead me, then, by the paths which He loves to travel. I shall be at the height of my joy provided that He is pleased. Then Jesus took me by the hand, and He made me enter a subterranean passage where it is neither cold nor hot, where the sun does not shine, and in which the rain or the wind does not visit, a subterranean passage where I see nothing but a half-veiled light, the light which was diffused by the lowered eyes of my Fiancé's Face! . . .

My Fiancé says nothing to me, and I say nothing to Him either except that *I love Him more than myself*, and I feel at the bottom of my heart that it is true, for I am more His than I am my own! . . . I don't see that we are advancing towards the summit of the mountain since our journey is being made underground, but it seems to me that we are approaching it without knowing how. The route on which I am has no consolation for me, and nevertheless it brings me all consolations since Jesus is the one who chose it, and I want to console Him alone, alone! . . .

◆ ◆ ◆

Before she entered Carmel, St. Thérèse had journeyed with her father and sister Céline on a pilgrimage to Rome. Most of the travel was done by train and St. Thérèse marveled at the beautiful countryside. We can imagine that train also passed through some tunnels in the mountains. This present letter, written a few years later, speaks not of a geographic journey, but of a spiritual one. The summit of the mountain of Love is an image in Carmelite spirituality especially developed by St. John of the Cross in his commentary on his poem *The Dark Night.* Like the journey described by Thérèse, the journey unveiled in *The Dark Night* is one taken in love. St. John of the Cross begins his poem with a description of a whole household fallen asleep. The occupant of this household finds the fact that no one else is conscious of her activities is a stroke of good luck. While everyone else is asleep, she can slip out and meet with her beloved without being disturbed.

There are some who look at uncomfortable and unfamiliar experiences in the spiritual life as things to be avoided or problems to be overcome. They presume wrongly that prayer should always make us feel good. They believe that deep prayer is affirming and validating. The moment they do not feel affirmed or validated, they presume that God has abandoned them or that they must have done something to disappoint Him. They believe that they have lost the approval of the Lord. This becomes especially problematic when a soul becomes overly anxious or discouraged. In such cases, it is easy to backslide and give up on prayer. This was a pattern that St. Teresa of Ávila struggled with for many years until the Lord brought her through this difficult grace—a grace John of the Cross calls the dark night and St. Thérèse understands as an underground passage up the mountain of Love.

St. John of the Cross describes the passageway up Mount Carmel as a way to be traveled by faith alone. To travel by any other way is to take the long way around. When we try to make progress according to whether we feel approved or have attained some other psychological state of consciousness, we are not progressing by faith alone and our journey will be circuitous. Thérèse, when describing allowing Jesus to show her the way, is not contradicting St. John of the Cross. The summit of the mountain of Love is not different than the summit of Mount Carmel. These are simply different names for the same place. Walking with Jesus is what St. John of the Cross means by going by faith alone. For him, faith is always animated by our living friendship with the Lord even when we cannot feel His presence, even when it feels like He has abandoned us.

St. Thérèse discloses a beautiful dimension of her own experience on this point. As she follows Christ and contemplates His face, what she describes is not consoling on the surface. The Bridegroom with whom she walks has lowered eyes. She beholds the Holy Face of the One who was crucified for her sake. She herself has taken up her cross and is following in His footsteps through the mysterious passageway that He forged to the summit of Love. The underground is an image of death—and as Thérèse is writing this letter, she is dying to herself and the only consolation she finds is contemplation of Christ Crucified. She cleaves to the conviction that the absence of consolation and approval that has closed in over her is not a form of rejection but rather a great grace. The dark passage through which she treads with her crucified lover provides a profound moment of solidarity with Him in which she is being purified and her love for Him is raised to new heights without her even being aware of it.

Love can take us to places where we otherwise would not have gone and into situations that we would have otherwise found inconvenient. When our devotion to Christ takes us into spiritual experiences with which we are unfamiliar and that we do not understand, we have entered into the journey of the Dark Night and into the heart of God. Many people equate the experience of night in the spiritual life with something negative. Some mistake it for some sort of spiritual desolation. Truth be told, any night, even those that are not so dark, never seems consoling. What brought us relief before and what was once a comfort is gone. But God does not want us to be attached to these lesser graces. They were only provided in the beginning to encourage us. This is why, when we are ready to grow, God takes away these lesser consolations. He can only give better and more wonderful graces in prayer when we let go of His lesser gifts. He is not content to give us good feelings or inspiring insights. He wants to give Himself. He desires that we possess Him in a union of true love.

One of the enemies of deep prayer is the temptation to be a little too self-aware of what we are doing and what we are experiencing. Instead of becoming bogged down in her difficult experience, Thérèse's attention is on the Lord. She is amazingly free of self-concern. Instead, her heart fixes on the Holy Face of her Beloved. In His face, she reads the greatness of His love and it pierces her to the heart. Mental prayer is all about this effort to allow our hearts to be pierced by the immensity of the love revealed in Christ's suffering. It is time where we allow the silence of Christ Crucified to resonate in our hearts. When we ponder His Passion for our sake, it is often the case that we leave meditation behind and we find ourselves plunged into the mystery of what He has done for us—even when this plunge does not feel consoling or understandable. For Thérèse, the mystery of Christ's face stirs deep desires in response. She longs to offer herself to Him the way that He offered Himself for her. In the light of His face, the difficult darkness of this night does not ultimately discourage her, but makes her want to love Him all the more: "I want to console Him alone, alone!"

DAY 9

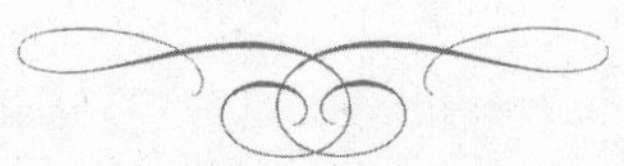

From Thérèse to Sr. Agnes of Jesus
September 3, 1890

Jesus does not look at time since there is no longer any time in heaven. He must look only at love. Ask Him to give me very much love too. I'm not asking for perceptible love, but a love felt only by Jesus. Oh! to love Him and make Him loved, how sweet this is! . . . Tell Him, too, to take me on the day of my Profession if I must still offend Him afterward, for I'd like to carry to heaven the white robe of my second Baptism without any stain on it. But, it seems to me, that Jesus can give me the grace of no longer offending Him or committing faults that *don't offend* Him but serve only to humble and make love stronger. If you only knew the things I'd tell you if I had the words to express what I am thinking, or rather what *I am not thinking* but feeling! . . . Life is very mysterious! . . . It is a desert and an exile . . . but at the bottom of my soul I feel that there will be a day of DISTANCES that will make me forget forever the sorrows of the desert and the exile. . . .

the little grain of sand

◆ ◆ ◆

The spiritual wisdom of St. Thérèse safeguards us against spiritual self-indulgence. She is an advocate for devotion that is not motivated by what we feel, but by what Christ feels. Awareness of the priorities of the Heart of the Lord over one's own hardships is a step toward spiritual maturity. At the same time, it is an act of profound confidence in God to allow oneself to be moved by the desires of the Lord for His own sake rather than for one's own. Those who are married will recognize this secret. What is true about love on a natural level is also the secret to a beautiful spiritual life. It is in the context of a nuptial love for Christ that Thérèse writes this letter to her older sister. It anticipates the first expressed desire of the Oblation to Divine Mercy, "to love Him and make Him loved."

Progress on the pathway of spiritual maturity is made by averting our attention from the difficult trials that we face and choosing instead what pleases the Lord in a given situation. This is a supreme act of trust because to really do this, we act, to some extent, against our own instincts of self-preservation. It is at this point we often wrestle with doubt. It might be expressed in the form of a question: Am I about to cross the line between a reasonable expression of devotion and one that is too zealous? This question is sometimes important to discuss with a spiritual director. Common sense is a gift from God and He expects us to make good use of it in our daily lives, but even so, a good spiritual director will help us consider how not even common sense is the ultimate norm in the spiritual life.

If we want to enter into union with God, the ultimate norm is total abandonment to love. This is the norm to which Jesus looks and this must be what we look to as well. Even on the natural level, parents will risk their lives for their children. Spouses often sacrifice themselves for each other out of devotion to their marriage. Similarly, our love for Christ often calls us beyond what seems reasonable and convenient and into a more radical and complete gift of self. Devotion to the Lord leads to what is uncomfortable and distasteful because we cannot love except at our own expense. If our love for God never involves sacrifice or renunciation or perseverance in difficult hardships, what good is it? Common sense is meant to support our efforts to love, and it is never meant to be an excuse for cowardice. To fully offer ourselves to the Lord in love means that we will need to find the courage to do something beautiful for Him.

◆ ◆ ◆

In this letter, we see that St. Thérèse is preparing for her religious profession with this kind of courage. She has in fact suffered difficult spiritual darkness and aridity. She feels as if she were in exile and not at home, even as she is about to enter community. Spiritually, Thérèse experiences dryness even as she is about to do something very beautiful for the Lord with her life. The mystery here is that instead of elation and excitement for her big day, she is aware of her sinfulness and aware that this second baptism—that is, her religious profession—can be an occasion of grace that changes her experience of sin.

◆ ◆ ◆

No matter how far we advance on the road of perfection in this life, we will always commit faults. When we are less mature, our failures can easily cause crises of faith and be the source of great shame and discouragement. We might even feel reluctant to go to Confession and take responsibility for our actions because we are so embarrassed about what we have done. Through this self-imposed isolation from the ministry of the Church and from those who could give us a word of hope, even a very small sin can cause us to backslide in big ways.

St. Thérèse proposes another way of dealing with our faults. There are faults that we commit and that we ought to confess, but that do not actually offend God. Even a venial sin only offends God to the extent that our charity becomes inert. But what if in the very moment that we acted in a way that diminished our love for God, He did something to re-ignite our love for Him? Such an act would not offend God but instead would be one more way for God to reveal the omnipotence of

His love at work in us. This approach to personal sin lives in the heart of the Oblation to Divine Mercy that Thérèse will compose and offer five years after writing this letter. It is not a matter of presumption but humility that allows her to contemplate her faults in this way, and this is a powerful example for us. Later, in her Oblation, she prays:

> If through weakness I sometimes fall,
> May your Divine Glance cleanse my soul immediately,
> Consuming all my imperfections like fire that transforms everything into itself.

Even more clearly than this letter, her Oblation attributes this new relationship to sin as a result of the purifying power of God's "Glance." This divine gaze on our sin consumes and transforms our failures like fire. Instead of separating us from the Lord, sin becomes an occasion that deepens our bond to Him when we humbly allow Him to look on what we have done.

St. Thérèse's self-offering takes us beyond isolated moments of sin and failure. To offer oneself the way she does in her Oblation involves the resolution to continually live under the purifying gaze of God, to allow the glance of His love to consume and transform our lives "incessantly." The reason why Thérèse can believe that God will act immediately through her faults to humble and strengthen her love is that she has already chosen to allow Him to do so in her weakness and even when she has sinned. Her trials have taught her how the power of God is brought to perfection in her weakness, and this gives St. Thérèse confidence that even when she sins, He is still at work; not only undaunted by her momentary lapse, but even utilizing it under the power of His loving gaze.

To truly make St. Thérèse's experience of personal sin something real for our own lives, we need to allow God to teach us humble receptivity to His love. Because of our inclination to avoid God's gaze in our lives, acquiring this kind of humility requires patient endurance of many hardships out of love for Him. Persevering in our devotion to God under difficult trials teaches us to humbly rely on Him because in them we confront the limits of our own self-sufficiency. This level of devotion under trial bears the fruit of spiritual stability and maturity. When our love is established in God through patient endurance, our occasional failures do not necessarily alienate us from Him or imprison us in paralyzing embarrassment. Free of self and alive for God, we are capable of a new and more surrendered vulnerability to His loving gaze. If we are humble and ready to take responsibility for our actions, our faults can be suddenly changed into occasions of grace like wood thrown onto a fire. The Sacrament of Confession is ordered toward this mystical reality, and through our contrition the Fire of God's love not only consumes our sins but also all the wounds that they have caused.

When in a moment of failure we are seized in a new way by the preciousness of the love of God, this is not a self-generated conscious state. It is the Holy Spirit using the occasion of our sin to lift up our hearts to God anew. He moves us to do whatever it takes not to let anything stand in the way of His love or our devotion to Him. Whenever this happens, we are experiencing how nothing can ever separate us from the love of God. We are drawn up beyond the hardships and trials and established forever in His presence. And He will seal this experience, which, after all, only anticipates the greater joy that the Lord has in store for those who love Him.

DAY 10

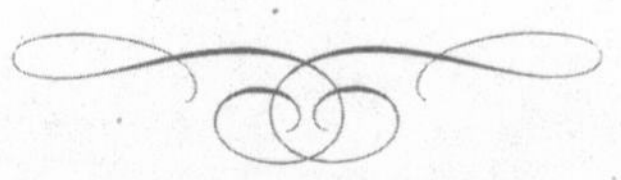

From Thérèse to Céline
July 8, 1891

Oh! what an exile it is, the exile of the earth, especially during these hours when everything seems to abandon us. . . . But it is then that it is precious, it is then that the day of salvation dawns; yes, dear Céline, suffering alone can give birth to souls for Jesus. . . . Is it surprising that we are so favored, we whose only desire is to save a soul that seems to be lost forever? . . . The details interested me very much, while making my heart beat very fast . . . But I shall give you some other details that are not any more consoling. The unfortunate prodigal went to Coutances where he started over again the conferences given at Caen. It appears he intends to travel throughout France in this way . . . Céline . . . And with all this, they add that it is easy to see that *remorse* is gnawing at him. He goes into church with a huge Crucifix, and he seems to be making great acts of adoration. . . . His wife follows him everywhere. Dear Céline, he is really culpable, more culpable than any other sinner ever who was converted. But cannot Jesus do once what He has not yet ever done? And if He were not to desire it, would He have placed in the heart of His poor little spouses a desire that He would not realize? . . . No, it is certain that He desires more than we do to bring back this poor stray sheep to the fold. A day will come when He will open his eyes, and then who knows whether France will not be traversed by him with a totally different goal from the one he has in mind now? Let us not grow tired of prayer; confidence works miracles. And Jesus said to Blessed Margaret Mary: "*One just soul* has so much power over my Heart that it can obtain pardon for a thousand *criminals*." No one knows if one is just or sinful, but, Céline, Jesus gives us the grace of feeling at the bottom of our heart that we would prefer to die rather than to offend Him; and then it is not our merits but those of our Spouse, which are *ours*, that we offer to Our Father who is in heaven, in order that our brother, a son of the Blessed Virgin, return vanquished to throw himself beneath the mantle of the most merciful of Mothers. . . .

◆ ◆ ◆

This letter introduces us to the great mystery of intercessory prayer in the Christian life. While other religious traditions believe that prayer is magical or even a therapeutic exercise, Catholic teaching is that prayer engages with the heart of God and thus truly changes the world. This vision of prayer is rooted in the Christian vision of God. God is the giver of all good gifts, and in His eternal plan, there are some gifts that He gives without ever having been asked and other gifts that He mysteriously withholds, prepared to generously give, when rightly asked. Prayer does not manipulate God or remind Him of a state of affairs that He does not already understand. Instead, prayer submits oneself, others, and whole situations to the loving mercy of God, and through an appeal to His mercy, it obtains real blessings that can transform everything.

We live in an era of the new evangelization and this pastoral effort should inform our prayer and attitudes towards those whom God has entrusted to us—especially those who have rejected God and stopped practicing their faith. Sometimes when we pray, we feel as if our intercession is a waste of time and believe that nothing is being accomplished. In such moments, the more we pray for someone who has backslid or renounced their faith, the more discouraged and anxious we become. Our intercession confronts our own impatience, our lack of capacity to stand firm with love and with confidence in God in the face of great sorrow. Although we might want the instant gratification of seeing the immediate results of divine action, God seems mysteriously inactive. We find ourselves confounded by the mysterious ways of providence.

Our resolve is sometimes undermined by the belief that the reason why God has not yet heard our prayer is that we have not figured out how to force Him to fix a situation. While it is good to study prayer and to practice spiritual exercises that others have found helpful, we must be very vigilant against the tendency to presume that God will give us what we want, the way we want, if only we use the right formula, method, or technique. In this letter, St. Thérèse's own effort to intercede reminds us that Love alone obtains graces for others in prayer.

St. Thérèse is concerned for the salvation of Hyacinthe Loyson, a Carmelite priest who abandoned his ministry, got married, and started his own church. Fr. Loyson preached all over the French countryside to promote his breakaway sect. While others viewed him with indignation, we know that St. Thérèse began to pray for "this poor stray sheep."

◆ ◆ ◆

During the spiritual trial she is suffering at the beginning of her Carmelite vocation, what is especially striking is that Thérèse finds in this hardship a deeper solidarity with Christ. In a journey that she does not understand—in what feels like exile and a desert—she begins to pray for a fallen-away priest. If his conversion seems completely unlikely, the saint wonders, "Cannot Jesus do once what He has not yet ever done?" To become an Oblation to Merciful Love like St. Thérèse requires that we adopt her simple attitude of humble faith concerning intercessory prayer. Her conviction concerning the ability of prayer to obtain graces that seem impossible is not based on her own spiritual accomplishments. Instead she knows that the outcome of prayer is rooted in the desires of the Lord's own heart ("He desires more than we do").

◆ ◆ ◆

Thérèse's living hope is deeply rooted in a profound reality of communion with the Lord. It is a matter of faith that Jesus has given Himself to us for our own possession. This means first of all that we possess His mysterious presence, even when we do not feel or understand it. It also means that we possess everything that belongs to Him in a way that we can use for His glory. This includes everything that He won for us on the Cross. His merits are our merits. We access these treasures by prayer and can evoke what He has done for our sake to obtain blessings from God. In her Oblation to Merciful Love, St. Thérèse will frame this truth about intercessory prayer in the words of Jesus:

> "Whatever you ask the Father in my name he will give to you!"
> I am certain, therefore, that you will grant my desires; I know it, O my God!
> The more you want to give, the more you make us desire.
> I feel in my heart immense desires and
> With confidence I ask you to come and take possession of my soul.

It is wrong to look at the merits of Christ in terms of quantitative reality. Instead, His merits are dynamic—that is, they produce something in those who receive them, so that the receivers become capable of offering prayer that is, as we say in the Mass, "right and just." To have faith in Jesus and to be devoted to Him means that we are open to everything that He longs to give us. And He wishes to give us everything that He merited for our sake. Prayer in the holy name of Christ renders our own prayer worthy in the eyes of the Father. Because of what Christ has done for us and because He has ascended to the right hand of the Father, Christ is able to offer our prayers to the Father, and the Father hears what we have asked for and gives it to us. This real access to God that Christ's work of redemption has opened up characterizes the nature of

Christian prayer and makes it an effective means of salvation, not only for ourselves, but also for those who we know need our prayer.

Prayer is part of a mysterious exchange of goods between God and humanity. Prayer works in the realm of grace and the sovereign freedom of the human heart. When we ask for our own salvation, contrite for our sins and ready to change our lives, God always grants our petitions if we persevere in faith. When we ask for the salvation of someone whom we have come to love, although God hears our prayers and pours out His grace in powerful ways, He also respects that soul's personal freedom. In the case of Fr. Loyson, some years after St. Thérèse died, a copy of this letter as well as *The Story of a Soul* were sent to him. He wrote that he was very moved by the letter but that it had not caused him to change his mind about his life or his decisions. However, he did hold out the possibility that he might be mistaken and if he was, he trusted in God's mercy. We do not know the ultimate fate of this soul for whom St. Thérèse shed many tears, but we do know that as he approached the Judgment Seat of God, he did so with the prayers of a saint who loved him. This is why we should always commend those the Lord places on our hearts to His merciful love without being overcome by anxiety or discouragement, but instead standing firm in humble faith.

DAY 11

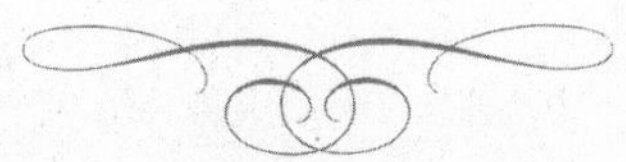

From Thérèse to Céline
October 19, 1892

JESUS HAS attracted us together, although by different way; together He has raised us above all the fragile things of this world whose image passes away. He has placed, so to speak, *all things* under our feet. Like Zacchaeus, we climbed a tree to see Jesus. . . . Then we could say with Saint John of the Cross: "All is mine, all is for me, the earth is mine, the heavens are mine, God is mine, and the Mother of my God is mine." With regard to the Blessed Virgin, I must confide to you one of my simple ways with her. I surprise myself at times by saying to her: "But good Blessed Virgin, I find I am more blessed than you, for I have you for a Mother, and you do not have a *Blessed Virgin to love*. . . . It is true you are the Mother of Jesus, but this Jesus has given you entirely to us . . . and He, on the Cross, He gave you to us as Mother. Thus we are richer than you since we possess Jesus and since you are ours also. Formerly, in your humility, you wanted one day to be the little servant of the happy Virgin who would have the honor of being the Mother of God, and here I am, a poor little creature, and I am not your servant but your child. You are the Mother of Jesus, and you are my Mother." No doubt, the Blessed Virgin must laugh at my simplicity, and nevertheless what I am telling her is really true! . . . Céline, what a mystery is our grandeur in Jesus. . . . This is all that Jesus has shown us in making us climb the symbolic tree about which I was just talking to you. And now what science is He about to teach us? Has He not taught us all? . . . Let us listen to what He is saying to us: "Make haste to descend, I must lodge today at your house." Well, Jesus tells us to descend. . . . Where, then, must we descend? Céline, you know better than I, however, let me tell you where we must now follow Jesus. In days gone by, the Jews asked our divine Savior: "Master, where do you live?" And He answered: "The foxes have their lairs, the birds have their nests, but I have no place to rest my head." This is where we must descend in order that we may serve as an abode for Jesus. To be so poor that we do not have a place to rest our head. This is, dear Céline, what Jesus has done in my soul during my retreat.

◆ ◆ ◆

When Thérèse entered Carmel, Céline shared with their father that she too wanted to join the Carmelite sisters. He was now physically and mentally disabled and institutionalized. The certitude about entering Carmel Céline once enjoyed was being put to the test. Her spiritual director attempted to influence her to take up an apostolate in Canada for almost a year.

Any test similar to what Céline experienced at this stage is important and involves discerning the most appropriate way of serving God in the midst of so many good works that could be done. This kind of discernment cannot be done on one's own and requires recourse to different forms of spiritual accompaniment. When she eventually enters Carmel, it is in part because of the letters that St. Thérèse wrote to her. This letter is one of many that helped Céline discern her vocation when it did not seem to make sense to her anymore.

At the heart of this beautiful letter is a special love that Thérèse enjoyed with her sister. Céline and Thérèse are bound together not only by blood but also by vocation. Now Céline's certitude is tested and Thérèse is the one who will help her find her way. It is to their reciprocal and authentic holy friendship that Thérèse appeals, and that friendship provides the basis for her to spiritually accompany Céline through this particular trial. Thérèse does not fully understand everything that Céline is suffering. In addition to the work in Canada that her spiritual director was encouraging her to consider, problems were being created for Céline by the priest who had discouraged Thérèse's entrance into Carmel. Her discouragement is compounded by the fact that she is not free to share everything she knows with her sisters. Finally, one last trial is added to her uncertainty and disappointment: something has happened to her life of prayer.

Not only external ambiguities but internal emptiness leave her feeling directionless. In August, Céline had written to her sister that she was not only unable to contemplate the vast horizons of God's love; it was hard for her to contemplate anything at all. She describes her prayer as passing through a series of voids or one long void. Céline is in a dark night, but Thérèse is coming out of one. Dawn had broken for Thérèse during the summer—not that she returned to earlier forms of consolation in prayer. Instead, God took away the former consolations to free St. Thérèse for an even deeper grace. Thérèse understands that Céline is walking this same path of faith and wants her sister to discover the more fully spiritual joy that she herself has found.

As she writes this letter, St. Thérèse knows from her own experience how arduous and necessary it is to travel this difficult void. To say that St. Thérèse had come out of this night is to say that she had begun to be accustomed to this new grace. In order to arrive at a deeper friendship with the Lord, she had to pass through a spiritual void in between the former way she enjoyed God's presence and a wholly new kind of joy. This new enjoyment of the Lord's personal presence was not a return to the good ol' days before the void. It was different, beckoning her into both a higher and a deeper awareness in faith.

Progress in holiness is made as we surrender former types of consolation we have received so that we might be completely and simply open to the new gifts that God wants to give. There is a state of spiritual shock that we must pass through when one kind of consolation in prayer is taken away. We suddenly find ourselves in a place where everything that used to make sense about God and His plan for our life is now taken away. It feels as if God has abandoned the soul. We continue without certitude about what God desires or whether we are included in His plan at all.

In truth, God is not less present, but more present to a soul that suffers these things in love. It is only because this greater presence of the Lord is unfamiliar that He does not seem present. Humble acceptance of this wholly new presence of God comes only by sober perseverance in love. Although she does not know all the details of Céline's plight, because of what she had just been through in her own spiritual life St. Thérèse is able to be insightfully compassionate. It is the perfection of holiness realized in love that raises them both up together above anything in the world that can stand in the way of love, and St. Thérèse wants her sister to understand it is by going into the depths of love that one becomes a dwelling place for God. To help Céline with this journey, St. Thérèse presents a seeming paradox with two movements of the soul that go in opposite directions. She speaks about an upward movement whereby the soul is above the difficult circumstances that oppose its progress. She also speaks about a downward movement in which we arrive at a deeper possession of Christ whose presence puts our present trials in their proper context.

This letter reflects a powerful new insight of which Thérèse begins to make use in order to spiritually accompany those whom she writes. Previously her reflections on the life of faith as an upward movement spoke about an ascent of the mountain of Love. Without contradicting this earlier image, this letter describes the ascent of faith and its descent in explicitly Gospel terms: the ascent and descent of Zacchaeus, who to find Jesus climbed a tree and to bring the Lord to his home had to climb down at Divine Command. Moreover, St. Thérèse understood the ascent as primarily a work accomplished by God, while the descent is an effort that God invites us to make.

◆ ◆ ◆

In her musings on the Blessed Virgin, St. Thérèse self-identifies with the Beloved Disciple and draws Céline into this self-identification. When she speaks about taking Mary as her mother, St. Thérèse is reminding Céline of Mary's special role in their lives. Céline and Thérèse lost their mother, St. Zélie Martin, when they were both young children. At the time, Louis Martin entrusted his daughters to Our Lady. Living out this entrustment to the Blessed Virgin, the girls came to understand that Jesus Himself had given His mother to them just as He had given her to His Beloved Disciple, John. Very early in their childhood, the girls took Mary into their hearts as their spiritual mother and grew up under the protection of her maternal presence, just as Christ Himself had.

Because Christ only gives beautiful gifts in beautiful ways, offering His mother to His Beloved Disciple from the Cross has a deep theological meaning for the spiritual life. From the Cross, Christ completely pours Himself out, showering us with an inexhaustible spiritual gift. To fully receive the gifts that He yearns for us to enjoy requires a special response from the very core of our being. The more we respond, the more He can give. This is true of the grace of forgiveness that is offered us from His fastened feet and His outstretched arms. If we accept forgiveness, our response must be expressed through a holy life. Our response to this total outpouring for our sake must be a prayerful life.

What about the gift of His mother that He offered His Beloved Disciple? Are we recipients of this gift too? For Thérèse, Christ's love revealed on the Cross not only evokes zeal for holiness and prayer, but also a special devotion to His mother. She takes His mother as her own mother. In doing this, Thérèse identifies with the Beloved Disciple, who stood with Mary at the foot of the Cross, and implies that Céline is in communion with her in this place of discipleship. What is true for Thérèse and Céline is true for each of us. Because Christ Crucified gives His mother to the disciple whom He loves, anyone who understands themselves as the beloved of Christ must also welcome Mary and love her as their own spiritual mother.

It would be reductionistic to think of this only on a sentimental level. Mary's spiritual motherhood in our lives of faith is a living reality. She intercedes for us because she is completely united to the mission of her Son. Accordingly, she has a key role in helping form devotion to Divine Mercy in our hearts. St. Thérèse helps us consider a certain aspect of this special role in a very creative way. She asserts that *she is more blessed* than the Blessed Virgin Mary. This assertion would seem at first to contradict Scripture passages recognize Mary as "full of grace" and "blessed among women" (Lk 1:28, 42). But St. Thérèse's simple argument is rooted in a logic that gives us pause. For all the honor and blessing that Mary enjoys in heaven, the Mother of God is not blessed with a mother as full of grace as Thérèse is able to claim. In accepting the gift of Mary from Jesus and taking her into her home to be her spiritual mother, this new relationship with the Mother of God is a gift that Mary herself cannot enjoy.

Here, St. Thérèse touches on the relational character of Christian mysticism. Great heights cannot be reached by overcoming one's humanity. Instead, what St. Thérèse sees is capable of lifting our humanity above difficulties is a new, personal relationship in the order of grace granted by God's generous gift. Our relationship with God also establishes us in the heavenly communion of saints. By humbly accepting all of God's gifts, especially the gift of His Mother, a soul is raised above the fray and into a higher existence. Through Mary, Thérèse understands that she and Céline have been lifted up to this spiritual height which gives new meaning to the voids they have passed through.

Day 11—Ascending and Descending with Christ

◆ ◆ ◆

In St. John of the Cross's *Dark Night of the Soul*, mystical contemplation is described as a secret ladder that one takes up into knowledge of God and that one takes down into knowledge of oneself. If in ascending it she identifies with the Beloved Disciple and glimpsed the immeasurable blessing we have in the spiritual mother Christ gives us, in descending St. Thérèse identifies with Zacchaeus, who came down to prepare a place for Christ to dwell at His command. The movement up involves a new realization of blessings that have been given. The movement down involves a sober awareness of one's own poverty obtained through obedient suffering.

Christ finds refreshment when we imitate the obedience that He learned by suffering (see Hebrews 5:8). This movement of obedience is profoundly connected to Christ's gift of Mary to us as our own spiritual mother. The Blessed Virgin's profession, "Let it be done to me," could only be uttered in anticipation of her Son's perfect prayer to the Father: "Your will be done." Just as the full meaning of Mary's yes is only revealed as she stands at the foot of the Cross, our own yes to God can only be fruitful when it leads us to humbly follow Christ Crucified.

He is the one who suffers extreme poverty: He has no place to lay His head. Only as we divest ourselves of everything in which we find rest do we enter into solidarity with Christ. It is only in our emptiness that the One who emptied Himself can find rest. This means that He is especially present in the void that loving obedience opens up in our hearts—the very same kind of void that Céline was suffering from when Thérèse wrote this message of hope. Céline is entering into the knowledge of Christ's presence that St. Thérèse names the "science of following Jesus." Thérèse leaves Céline, and us, with a word of encouragement as we pass through spiritual voids. We must pass through emptiness in order to prepare a place for Christ to abide. Thus, such crushing moments in prayer and in life are actually hidden and mysterious blessings. Thérèse is able to offer this encouragement to her sister in a compelling way because it is precisely what she herself had passed through.

DAY 12

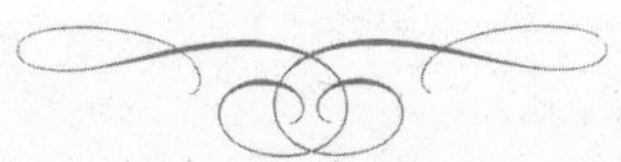

From Thérèse to Céline
October 20, 1893

Jesus is the one who must be our divine link. He alone has the right to penetrate the sanctuary of His spouse's heart. . . . Oh, yes! *He alone* understands when nothing answers us. . . . *He* alone arranges the events of our life of exile. It is He who offers us at times the bitter chalice. But we do not see Him, He is hiding. He veils His divine hand, and we can see only creatures. Then we suffer since the voice of our Beloved does not make itself heard and that of creatures seems to misunderstand us. . . . Yes, the most bitter sorrow is that of not being understood. . . . But this sorrow will never be Céline's or Thérèse's, never, for their eyes see higher than the earth, they are raised above what is created. The more Jesus hides Himself, the more, too, they feel that Jesus is close to them. With *exquisite delicacy*, He walks before them, throwing aside the stones on the road, removing the reptiles, and this is not all. He makes the voices of friends resound in our ears; these voices warn us not to walk with too much security. . . . And why? Is not Jesus the one who has traced out our route Himself? Is He not the one who enlightens us and reveals Himself to our souls? . . . Everything brings us to Jesus. The flowers growing on the edge of the road do not captivate our hearts; we gaze on them, we love them, for they speak to us about Jesus, about His power, about His love, but our souls remain free. Why disturb our sweet peace in this way? Why fear the storm when the heavens are serene?

. . . Oh, Céline! my dear Céline. . . . it is not the precipices we must avoid, we are in the arms of Jesus, and if the voices of friends advise us to fear, it is our Beloved who *wills it* so, and why? . . . Ah! in His love He chooses for His spouses the same road He chose for Himself. . . . He wills that the purest joys be changed into sufferings so that not having, so to speak, even the time to breathe at ease, our heart may turn to Him who alone is our Sun and our joy. . . .

The *flowers by the roadside* are the *pure pleasures* of life. There is no evil whatsoever in enjoying them, but Jesus is *jealous* of our souls, He desires that all pleasure be mingled with bitterness for us. . . . And yet the *flowers on the roadside* lead to the Beloved, but they are a roundabout way, they are the plaque or the mirror reflecting the Sun, but they are not the Sun itself.

◆ ◆ ◆

Before she entered Carmel, Céline suffered from not being fully understood by either the Carmelites or the family members with whom she was living. She experienced two seemingly conflicting passions: her passion for the Carmelite vocation and her passion as an aspiring artist. Everyone closest to her believed that she had to choose one or the other, and they did not understand how an artistic soul might also have a religious contemplative vocation, or vice versa. Her spiritual director in a letter to Thérèse at about this same time implies that Céline is suffering greatly. In a letter written several months earlier in the same year, Céline describes herself as numb and like a cloud. She remarks that her only faithful companion is Tom, her dog. With this in mind, we can assume that this letter was probably intended to offer a word of hope to Céline.

◆ ◆ ◆

The basic message to Céline is that the artistic gift she has is a pure joy; something in her life that pleases God. Borrowing imagery from the poetry of St. John of the Cross, Thérèse refers to these pure joys in life as flowers along the way. In the poem *Spiritual Canticle* the Bridegroom has planted and strewn all manner of beautiful flowers along the pathway on which His bride follows Him. He did so not that they should distract or delay the Bride, but that these flowers might make her journey more beautiful. St. Thérèse sees Céline's love for painting as one of these beautiful flowers.

Having so recently emerged from her own dark night, St. Thérèse is experientially aware of how to not be distracted by the flowers in our progress to union with Him. She knows that God permits some sorrow to be strewn in among the pure joys of life. The gifts themselves are not displeasing to Him, but instead, He permits our pure joys to be mixed with sorrow only to the extent that doing so will hasten our pursuit of Him as the fulfillment of all desire. He wants the soul to quicken its devotion and not be dissipated by pursuits that will hold it back from progress. Indeed the pure joys of life distract us precisely because they are from God who, being so Beautiful, can only give extraordinarily beautiful gifts.

He is aware of how fickle we are and how we are made for something much more than even the most wondrous of His gifts in the natural order. This is why He permits all kinds of trials and difficulties in souls for whom He has a special affection. Difficult trials are the way that He reorients our relationship to everything in our lives so that we might find Him in everything.

The loneliness and misunderstanding that have distressed Céline are bitter and numbing. St. Thérèse is attempting to reassure her sister that what God has permitted is actually quite freeing, if she will accept it. When a soul is not detained by lower pursuits, it is more dedicated to the higher calling that it has received. In other words, Thérèse understands the sorrow that her sister is suffering. Caught between her love of painting and religious life, Céline is being invited to a deeper trust in Jesus—even to surrender her love of painting to Him. Why? Because the Lord has something so much more beautiful to give to her: namely, the gift of His own presence in a very intimate way. Such is the grace of consecrated contemplative life. St. Thérèse wants Céline to be open to this joy.

What is true in this vocation is true for all Christians: Christ is the answer to the feelings of loneliness and of not being understood. He is consolation in the face of every sorrow and difficult choice. When we travel by faith we are always in His arms, no matter how difficult the pathway becomes. Thérèse's spiritual counsel is rooted in a great truth: we are never really alone, and at the end of the day there is Someone who understands us even better than we understand ourselves. This Someone is Christ, the Bridegroom of our souls, who never abandons us even when we do not feel or sense His presence, even when we suffer feelings of alienation and find ourselves disconnected from those we most love. St. Thérèse gets to this truth by describing Christ as our divine link and as the one who has the authority to penetrate our hearts.

Jesus is the mediator. In the perfect unity of humanity and divinity realized in His Divine Person, He links us to God. He also links us together in solidarity with one another. Even when those we love and rely on misunderstand us, He is able to create the connection that we need. The solidarity that He makes real surpasses our natural relationships, limited as they are by the frail scope of mere human empathy. Instead, His personal presence heals, purifies, and intensifies our humanity even when this divine presence is unfamiliar and unperceived.

This presence of Jesus penetrates the heart even when we do not understand ourselves. Christ Crucified is able to pierce our hearts because we pierced His first. His Passion and death have won His sacred humanity access to the sanctuary of heaven as well as the sacred space of each person's innermost being. With the authority of this merciful love, He searches the depths of the soul that even the soul itself cannot reach. Our Merciful Savior knows us better than we know ourselves and is always ready to suffer those secret sorrows that weigh down the soul. Every soul is filled with these difficult sorrows. Each faces them or runs away from them, but there has never been a soul that must suffer its sorrow alone. The Living God is already pierced to the heart by the soul's plight and with divine omnipotence is fully present to the inner misery that places the dignity of His son or daughter at risk. He waits for us to trust Him with what weighs us down and to surrender to Him what we are trying to bear alone.

◆ ◆ ◆

The presence of the Risen Lord dawns in our loneliness when we are willing to seek Him there. St. Thérèse points to this truth when she observes that the more He is hidden, the more He is felt. The kind of feeling she is describing is not stirred on the level of natural perception but on the infinitely higher level of faith. It is a particular feeling born of belief and stirred by the beautiful gentleness with which God prefers to work in a soul.

St. Thérèse is not counseling her sister to try to feel God's presence, but to believe in it. If Céline feels she is like a cloud, Thérèse knows that God is still present in ways that go far beyond the limits of our feelings, understanding, intuition, and even our imagination. To believe that God is present in this way is to be vulnerable to a wholly unfamiliar mystery. In such faith, our understanding, intuition, and imagination are all touched even without our realization. The very core of our being wakes to love while we are yet unaware. In this beautiful spiritual space "everything" brings us Jesus. This is what Thérèse has experienced and this is what she wants for Céline.

St. Thérèse is already beginning to form Céline spiritually to make a special offering of her life to the merciful love of the Lord. To be authentic, the offering of ourselves as a victim to the merciful love of Jesus requires special preparation. On the one hand, it takes a dedication of ourselves to the daily discipline of Christian living and to ongoing conversion of heart. It also requires perseverance in the face of difficult hardships, especially in those moments where nothing makes sense anymore, when we feel lost in a cloud.

The Lord is helping us raise our eyes from the flowers on the pathway to seek the One from whom they came. He is the One who will teach us to make a perfect act of love. He is the One who will lead us to Himself. He is the One who will help us save our brothers and sisters and who will help us make His merciful love known to the world.

DAY 13

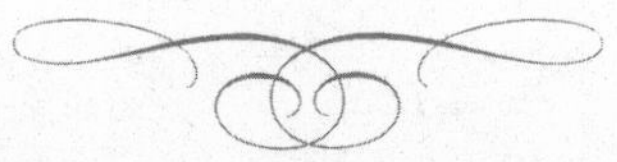

From Thérèse to Céline
July 18, 1894

I AM NOT surprised at your trials; I passed through this *last year* and I *know what it is*! . . . God willed that I make my sacrifice; I made it and now, like you, I have felt calm in the midst of suffering.

But I felt something else, that frequently God wants only *our will*; He asks *all*, and if we were to refuse Him the least thing, He loves us too much to give in to us; however, as soon as our will is conformed to His, as soon as He sees we seek Him alone, then He conducts Himself with us as in the past He conducted Himself with Abraham. . . . This is what Jesus is making me feel interiorly, and I think that you are on TRIAL, that *now* the cutting off is taking place which you feel is necessary. . . . It is *now* that Jesus is *breaking* your *nature*, that He is giving you the cross and tribulation. The more I go on, the more I have the inner certitude that one day you will come here. . . .

You perhaps believe I do not understand you? . . . And I assure you that I am reading into your soul. . . . I read that you are faithful to Jesus, willing only His will, *seeking only His love; fear nothing. In the present trial* God is purifying what might be too human in our affection, but the *foundation* itself of the affection is too pure for Him to break it. Listen well to what I am going to say to you. Never, never, will Jesus separate us. If I die before you, do not believe I shall be far from your *soul*, never shall we have been more united! It is perhaps this which Jesus wills to make you feel when speaking to you of separation? But, above all, do not worry, I am not sick; on the contrary, I have iron health, however, God can break iron just like clay. . . .

◆ ◆ ◆

"I am not surprised by your trials," Thérèse writes. A good spiritual director is someone who is a few steps ahead of us in the pathway of faith. Such spiritual accompaniment is able to help us recognize the nature of the trials we are facing because another has also experienced them and sees them now from the other side. Such a soul is able to speak a word of hope and help us find our way. This is what St. Thérèse offers to her sister Céline.

In yesterday's reflection we talked about how the Lord might use loneliness and misunderstanding to help us rethink our heart's priorities. In this letter, Thérèse's wisdom helps us see that those who persevere through trials with faith are able to love with greater purity and intensity than they had ever known before. Offering ourselves as an Oblation to Merciful Love requires that we allow the Lord to intensify and refine our existence in this way.

Is it true that Jesus breaks our nature? In Romans 6, St. Paul explains that we are baptized into Christ's death. He later explains that he no longer lives his own life, but the life of Christ in him (Gal 2:20). Because something natural to Paul has been put to death, something new is born in him. This is what it means to renounce ourselves, pick up our cross, and follow our crucified God. This teaching is important in the wisdom of the Carmelite Doctors of the Church. For St. Teresa of Ávila, a radical detachment from human affection is necessary if we are to find union with the Lord. This was a fierce struggle for her until, through a special grace in prayer, she was pierced to the heart by the fire of God's love.

For St. John of the Cross, one is not really a friend of the Lord if one refuses to spiritually imitate His death on the Cross. Indeed, Christ, he argues, not only suffered death in His physical body, but also the annihilation of his very spirit in so far as He felt abandoned by the Father. He quotes the psalm that Jesus prayed in his Passion, "My God, my God, why have you forsaken me?"

Following in the footsteps of John and Teresa, Thérèse encourages Céline to understand their own friendship in this light. It suggests that they both had to let go of a certain natural bond with each other so that they might be open to a new spiritual bond of friendship. We have already seen that, whereas before she entered religious life Céline had a maternal role in Thérèse's life, now, in the order of grace, Thérèse has a spiritually maternal role in the life of Céline. She is teaching her sister the way to union with God. Thérèse, however, highlights a truth for Céline that is only latent in the teachings of John and Teresa. Although we suffer a spiritual death in our union with Christ, this death does not destroy what is most true, good, and noble about us. The Lord does not destroy the foundations of love when they are pure.

It is exactly for all that is true, good, and noble in our dignity that Christ came and died for us. Whatever is evil and vicious in our lives died with Him on the Cross. Whatever is good and virtuous in humanity was raised up with Him from the dead. Thérèse is reassuring Céline that although the grace of Christ purifies what is not noble in our relationships, this same grace heals and restores everything that is good and true in them.

The beautiful thing about the spiritual relationships that God establishes is that they are more powerful than death. Thérèse explains to Céline that even if she dies, Jesus will not separate them, but only make them all the more close. Thérèse has no idea how quickly her death will come. Yet the truth that she shares with her sister anticipates this difficult trial. Death cannot overtake the love of Christ unleashed in us. It is powerless to break the bonds that He establishes among those who believe in Him and who are being made perfect in love. So then, there is nothing to fear. We can have every confidence in the love of Christ at work in us.

As we grow more confident in this love, our hearts become more open to new friendships. As we offer our lives moment-by-moment as living sacrifices to the mercy of God, we are able to help our friends make a gift of their own lives to the merciful love of God. The Oblation to Divine Mercy then is a very relationship-based reality that teaches us that the mystery of friendship cannot be contained in this life on earth alone.

DAY 14

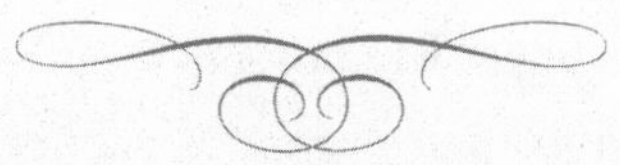

From Thérèse to Céline
August 19, 1894

I AM very happy, dear little Céline, that you are not experiencing any perceptible attraction in coming to Carmel. This is a favor from Jesus, who wills to receive a *gift* from you. He knows it is much sweeter to give than to receive. We have only the short moment of this life *to give* to God . . . and He is already preparing to say: "Now, my turn. . . ." What a joy to suffer for Him who loves us unto *folly* and to pass as *fools* in the eyes of the world. We judge others as we judge ourselves, and since the world is senseless, it naturally thinks we are the ones who are senseless! . . . But, after all, we are not the first; the only crime with which Jesus was reproached by Herod was that of being *foolish*, and I think like him! . . . Yes, it was *folly* to seek out the poor little hearts of mortals to make them His *thrones*, He, the King of Glory, who is seated above the Cherubim . . . He, whom the heavens cannot contain. . . . He was *foolish*, our Beloved, to come to earth in search of sinners in order to make them His friends, His intimates, His *equals*, He, who was perfectly happy with the two adorable Persons of the Trinity! . . . We shall never be able to carry out the follies He carried out for us, and our actions will never merit His name, for they are only very rational actions and much below what our love would like to accomplish. It is the world, then, that is senseless since it does not know what Jesus has done to save it, it is the world which is a *monopolizer*, which seduces souls, and which leads them to springs without water. . . .

We are not *idlers*, squanderers, either. Jesus has defended us in the person of the Magdalene. He was at table, Martha was serving, Lazarus was eating with Him and His disciples. As for Mary, she was not thinking of taking any food but of *pleasing* Him whom she loved, so she took a jar filled with an ointment of great price and poured it on the *head* of Jesus, after *breaking the jar*, and the whole house was scented with the ointment, but the APOSTLES *complained* against Magdalene. . . . It is really the same for us, the most fervent *Christians*, *priests*, find that we are *exaggerated*, that we should *serve* with Martha instead of consecrating to Jesus the *vessels* of our *lives*, with the ointments enclosed within them. . . . And nevertheless what does it matter if our *vessels* be broken since Jesus is *consoled* and since, in spite of itself, the world is obliged *to smell* the perfumes that are exhaled and serve to purify the empoisoned air the world never ceases to breathe in.

◆ ◆ ◆

In this letter, St. Thérèse helps us see how consecrated contemplative life, life set apart for the Lord through a rigorous commitment to prayer, is not to be compared to other vocations simply on the basis of its apparent usefulness. We tend to think that one vocation is just as good as another or that vocations of service to the community are more useful than vocations given to prayer and solitude. This may be true in a certain sense. Wherever God has placed us and whatever He has moved us to say yes to is a wondrous thing. At the same time, the more radically we respond to Him, the more our response to His call reflects the radical way that He has acted toward us.

In a very beautiful and mysterious way, those who choose consecrated life have made the most beautiful offering of themselves to God that is possible in the Church. Part of the drama of their vocation is their faithfulness to the Lord in the midst of ambiguity, loneliness, and mental anguish. Their example to us is worth meditating on in order to examine how in our own lives we too should respond to God in our hardships. Their faithfulness in their devotion is a living sign of what heaven is all about. They help us realize that heavenly life is not in the remote future, but anticipated already in the present moment by faith.

In this letter, Thérèse counsels her sister to persevere in pursuing a deep desire that has been with her since childhood. Céline, who is older than Thérèse, had also desired to enter Carmel with her other sisters very early on. She suspended her own plans to help her younger sister enter at an even earlier age. It was a sacrificial act to encourage and facilitate Thérèse's entry first. Yet Céline did so with maternal affection for her younger sister. Now the circumstances for Céline to enter are favorable. She is on the verge of embracing a way of life that she has longed to experience for so many years. Suddenly, however, she finds herself without any attraction to it. St. Thérèse wants Céline to see this moment of ambiguity as another opportunity to express her love for Jesus in an even more radical way.

St. Louis Martin died just a few weeks before this letter was written. Céline immediately shared with the superior at Carmel her desire to enter. She also revealed her spiritual director's plans about her taking on missionary work in Canada to her sisters. The external circumstances do not allay her internal turmoil. At the time of this letter, Céline has been plagued with second thoughts and even nightmares about the reality that she has chosen. She has come to question the validity of her desire to enter Carmel to rejoin her sisters as a religious nun. Is it foolishness after all?

Thérèse answers Céline's doubt by turning her attention to the foolishness of God. If being a consecrated contemplative nun is foolish, Thérèse asks her to consider how foolish God has been in His love for us. The logic of Thérèse's answer revolves around the immensity of

God's love. In the Oblation to Merciful Love, Thérèse refers to floods of tenderness and kindness waiting to break forth. God does not calculate His response to us. He is ready to respond in ways that exceed anything that would make sense. The excessiveness or foolishness of His love is revealed definitively on the Cross. St. Thérèse recognizes in Céline's doubts the unfolding of this same mystery and the opportunity for Céline to become implicated in it. Doubt becomes, in the counsel of St. Thérèse, not an obstacle, but another opportunity to return the love we have already received from God in a manner that is in some way commensurate to what He has given in giving Himself to the end.

This is why Thérèse believes that Céline is only having this trial because Christ wants her to know a greater joy. Thérèse learned years before how the joy that one has in loving without return is greater than the joy one has in simply being loved. She speaks into Céline's doubt about the wisdom of her decision. St. Thérèse's answer is simple: To foolishly respond to the love of God is simply to love Him the way He loves us.

Her use of Mary of Bethany's devotion to Christ is beautiful for us to think about (see Jn 12:2–8). Today, Scripture scholars have helped us more carefully distinguish between Mary of Bethany, the sister of Lazarus who washed Jesus' feet with her tears and later anointed His head with oil, and Mary Magdalene, whom Jesus liberated from demonic possession and to whom He appeared after the Resurrection (see Lk 8:2). Yet, at the time of Thérèse, these stories were read into each other, and the composite of Mary of Bethany and Mary Magdalene became a symbol of the contemplative life. Using this hermeneutic, Thérèse applies this passage to the doubts troubling Céline.

What was true at the end of the nineteenth century continues to be true today: contemplative life is believed to be less useful than the active life. Contemplatives themselves are often considered foolish idlers even more today than they were at the time of St. Thérèse. In particular, the social and psychological idealism that emerged in the Industrial Revolution of Thérèse's day are still very much at play in our own technocracy. Only today, we allow technology to create a vacuum in our souls so that the fullness of contemplative living is even more repulsive to us than it once was. We have become so addicted to noise and amusement that we are now hostile to silence and everything that is simply human. We cannot even conceive of life without all of this important noise.

To dispel these appearances for Céline and for us, Thérèse focuses on how Mary, who was accused of being idle and too extravagant, broke an expensive jar of perfume for no other reason than to console Jesus. In referring to the broken jar, Thérèse knows that Céline is not just having second thoughts, but feels like she is breaking apart. She is the costly jar. Her life is the perfume. Others will not understand what she is offering. Thérèse is reassuring: even when life feels shattered, Jesus is worthy of our total dedication to Him. The reassurance has a lasting effect on Céline, who enters Carmel as Sr. Marie of the Sacred Heart.

The Act of Oblation to Merciful Love to which our reflections are ordered is also about breaking an expensive jar of perfume. This jar and perfume is the pouring out of our own lives in union with the offering of Christ crucified. It is a foolish offering filled with the wisdom of God. As we renew the Act of Oblation to Merciful Love each day, we are also opening ourselves to this same mystery of God's love. This oblation urges us beyond our own feelings and empowers us to choose to love God extravagantly in the moment. This self-offering is in opposition to the vacuum that unrestrained recourse to amusement and technology can create in our hearts. This gift requires a contemplative disposition and the renunciation of clamor and meaningless distraction in our lives.

While not everyone is called to enter consecrated life, those who have consecrated their lives to God are living signs of the foolish devotion and love that we owe Him. As a living sign, a consecrated person points to something beyond what we can see and measure in this world. They have chosen not to put their identity in what they possess or achieve, but in Christ who emptied Himself and in what He has achieved. They have given up marriage and family to help build up the family of God. In the anonymity, silence, and secret sacrifices to which their whole existence is ordered, they lift our hearts to a higher reality that is immeasurable and invisible.

Whatever our own vocation, above the day-to-day struggles and above the ambiguities we confront, God's love reigns supreme. To offer ourselves as an Oblation to His Merciful Love is to accept the supremacy of His love and to ground our whole existence in it. Our brothers and sisters in religious life are living icons of this mystery. Yet, it is a mystery into which everyone who loves God and desires others to know His saving love are drawn together.

DAY 15

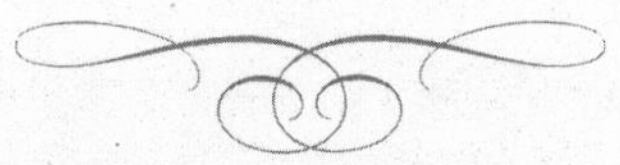

From Thérèse to Sister Thérèse-Dosithee (Léonie)
January 1895

DEAR LITTLE SISTER, do you not find, as I do, that our Father's departure has brought us close to heaven? More than half of the family now enjoys the vision of God, and the five exiles on earth will not be long in flying away to their homeland. This thought of the brevity of life gives me courage, it helps me bear with the weariness of the road. What does a little work on earth matter (says the *Imitation [of Christ*]) . . . we pass away and we have not here a lasting dwelling! Jesus has gone before us to prepare a place in the home of His Father, and then He will come and He will take us with Him so that where He is we also may be. . . . Let us wait, let us suffer in peace, the hour of rest is approaching, the light tribulations of this life of a moment are preparing us for an eternal weight of glory. . . .

Dear little Sister, how much your letters pleased me and did *some good to my soul.* I rejoice when seeing how much God loves you and is granting you His graces. . . . He finds you worthy of suffering for His love, and it is the greatest proof of affection that He may give you, for suffering makes us like Him. . . .

◆ ◆ ◆

Léonie has travelled a very difficult road to find her vocation. She has gone in and out of religious life. For a time, she lived at home with Céline to take care of their father. But after the death of St. Louis Martin and after Céline entered Carmel, Léonie attempted religious life again. In January of 1895 Leonie was a religious sister at the Monastery of the Visitation, which she left in July of that same year. She is the only living sibling not in the Carmel at Lisieux. Her vocation continues to be a struggle and Thérèse, instead of advising her, thanks her for her good encouragement. They are two souls who understand suffering, and the death of their father has bound them even closer.

A beautiful theme of this letter is the spiritual good of meditating on just how brief and uncertain this life really is (see Psalm 39:4). Without this reference point, our instinct for self-preservation often limits our capacity to be patient. It is easy, at this point, to lessen our devotion and even to become careless about our practices. When we step back, however, and re-evaluate our judgments and actions under the light of the brevity of life, we are gently reminded of the goal of our striving and we find the courage to "not grow weary" in doing what is right (Gal 6:9). Shadows that seemed so heavy when they preoccupied our minds are suddenly lighter in the dawn of heaven's brightness.

Léonie has written a letter that validates this thought for Thérèse. For those who have not lost someone whom they deeply loved, it is too easy to skip over this thought, or else to fail to allow the dynamism of Thérèse's perspective to resound in the heart. A certain solitude envelops us after we lose our parents. The heart aches with desire to be reunited again. Léonie and Thérèse have suffered losing both of their parents, and Léonie has also given up, out of devotion to Christ, the physical fellowship of her sisters. Yet, they have chosen the pathway of faith out of love for the Lord who has prepared a place "in the home of the Father" for them.

Their sorrow is not without hope. Though they are separated from one another geographically, their hearts converge on the desire for heaven and this same desire provides a context for their current trials. The solidarity of faith is greater than any physical distance. Nor can death break this deep bond. Now, because of their saintly father, they have a heavenly vision of this present life, its duration, and where they can find their rest.

It is in this context of faith in the face of death that we can begin to understand St. Thérèse's mysterious words about "suffering for His Love" as "a proof of Divine Affection." St. Thérèse understands that the Lord's special love for a soul is proven when He permits it to suffer for His love. God is the one whose tenderness and kindness are shut up within His mystery, waiting to burst forth. Only a soul that suffers for His love can satisfy His desire that the world might realize how loved it really is. At the same time, only a soul willing to suffer this love in the present moment really understands the deep things of God. As it strives to make His love known in the situation it confronts, a soul is vulnerable to the painfully beautiful but hidden mystery of His merciful love. To suffer this divine love is to in some sense be like Him, and this likeness is the very basis of a true friendship with the Lord.

This is not true in every kind of suffering. When we torment ourselves about what would have or could have been we are not glorifying God. His love is not found in feeling sorry for ourselves or indulging in self-pity. Neither is there anything meritorious in replaying old injuries or grievances in our minds. Nursing bitterness over injury and wallowing in righteous indignation are sins that grieve the heart of the Lord. Instead, it is only in suffering *for the love of God* that special proof of divine favor is realized.

Léonie's "suffering for love" is at the heart of St. Thérèse's Act of Oblation to the Merciful Love of God. At the time, neither Thérèse nor Léonie could have possibly imagined the wonderful work that God was accomplishing as they dealt with the death of their father. Because of the power of God's love at work in her sorrow, Léonie is being given the opportunity to make a special offering of herself to God for love and by love. As she does this, she gives to God a new and mysterious way to reveal His tender friendship. A deep solidarity with God's merciful love is opened up. This loving movement toward a deeper solidarity with the Lord coincides with what St. Thérèse articulates as her Act of Oblation.

Very specifically, our nineteenth-century Doctor of the Church connects her oblation with a "holocaust" offering. This is strong language. For her a holocaust is a complete spiritual sacrifice of one's very existence to God for love and by love. Difficult trials, like the one Léonie now faces, do not thwart, but instead occasion this kind of sacrifice. Pondering the nature of this offering as a spiritual holocaust, we find delicate reassurance that persevering in our devotion to the Lord and in our service to one another in the midst of trial is meaningful and not diminished even in the face of death.

Holocaust offerings and the mercy of God have rich biblical significance: the peace that only God's mercy provides requires both sacrifice and faith. In the Book of Leviticus, a holocaust is an actual animal sacrifice. Unlike other sacrifices, the holocaust was completely consumed by the sacred flame before the presence of God as a total offering. As an expression of trust in the mercy of God, this total offering evoked the same faith that made Abraham righteous before God. A holocaust was meant to be a renewal of this faith and presented a new opportunity for the Lord to reveal His mercy.

In the New Covenant, Christ made this offering not through the symbol and sign of an animal, but by giving up His own life for our sake (see Hebrews 9:12). In this holocaust, He is both the Lamb of God and our Great High Priest. He was not consumed by material fire. Instead, with the fire of God's love, He was lifted on high. In permitting Himself to be completely consumed by the love of the Father for us, He has offered Himself in a way that enables Him to raise us also to the dignity of sharing in this redemptive work. It is on the basis of the possibility of our participation in Christ's redemptive work that St. Thérèse can call the Act of Oblation to Merciful Love a holocaust—it is a sharing in Christ's sacrifice of Himself on the Cross.

By faith and Baptism, we are joined to the Lord's saving mystery (see Romans 6:3–4). Our faith, especially in times of difficulties, joins us to Christ's work of redemption and extends its power through our lives and into the circumstances that we bear out of love for His sake. When we abandon ourselves to the love of God out of trust and devotion, our lives are transformed into a unique gift of divine love for the world. St. Paul calls this "a living sacrifice, . . . your spiritual worship" (Rom 12:1). The total holocaust that Christ offered for our sake on the Cross is an oblation that we renew through our own efforts to be patient in the midst of trials.

DAY 16

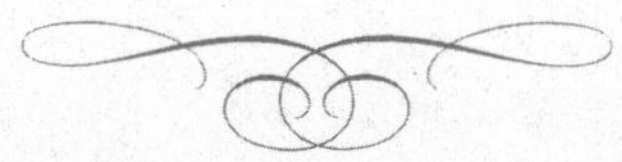

From Thérèse to Mme. Guérin
July 20, 1895

I CAN TELL you something which you must not tell Uncle because he would love me no longer, this thing you know better than I. It is that he is a saint such as are few on earth and his faith can be compared to that of Abraham. . . . Ah! if you only knew with what sweet emotion my soul was filled yesterday when seeing him with his angelic little Marie. . . . We were plunged into a very great sorrow because of our dear Léonie, it was like a real agony. God, who willed to try our faith, was sending us no consolation whatever, and, as for me, I was unable to offer any other prayer but that of Our Lord on the Cross: "My God, my God, why have you abandoned us!" Or like that in the garden of agony: "My God, may Your will be done and not ours," Then to console us, our divine Savior did not send us the angel who sustained Him in Gethsemane but one of His *saints*, still a traveler on earth and filled with His divine strength. When we saw his calm, his resignation, our anxieties were dispelled, we felt the support of a paternal hand. . . . Oh, dear little Aunt! how great are God's mercies on His poor children! . . . If you only knew the sweet tears I shed when listening to the heavenly conversation of my holy Uncle. . . . He seemed to me already transfigured, his language was not that of a faith that hopes but of a love that possesses. At the moment when trial and humiliation came to visit him, he appeared to forget everything in order to think of nothing but to bless the divine hand which was taking from him his *Treasure*, and, as a *reward*, was testing him like a saint. . . . St. Teresa was very right in saying to Our Lord, who was loading her with crosses when she was undertaking great works for Him: "Ah! Lord, I am not surprised that You have so few friends; You treat them so badly!" On another occasion, she said that the souls whom God loves with an ordinary love He gives some trials, but on those He loves with a love of predilection He lavishes His crosses as the most certain mark of His tenderness.

◆ ◆ ◆

The letters that we have reflected on so far precede and lead up to the Oblation to Merciful Love that St. Thérèse spontaneously offered on the Solemnity of the Holy Trinity, June 9, 1895. She then wrote down the words that she offered at Mass from her heart. After a little discernment, her oldest sister, Marie of the Sacred Heart, will join her in this offering a few weeks later. This letter to their mother's sister, their aunt Céline Guérin, is written closely following this special offering.

Céline Guérin's daughter Marie and Thérèse are very close and, in fact, Marie will join the Carmel in Lisieux within weeks of this letter. Having lived with them after the death of her mother, Thérèse believed that her Aunt and Uncle Guérin were saints and said so in this letter in a very playful way. Yet, this letter is inseparable from the letter to Léonie we just reflected on. It addresses a very painful moment for the Martin and Guérin families. Seeing her uncle and her cousin Marie just before they left to bring Léonie home seems to have occasioned this letter from St. Thérèse to her aunt. Though she tried, Léonie was not able to persevere in religious life with the Visitation Sisters. This is Léonie's second failed attempt. Thérèse knows that this is an embarrassment for her sister as well as for her aunt's family who has already been an object of local gossip. This message is written out of gratitude for her aunt and uncle's continued solicitude for their niece.

Day 16—A Love That Possesses

Just as Thérèse observed in our last reflection, God found Léonie worthy of suffering, and Léonie felt she was past her breaking point. Even when Thérèse was writing her, Léonie was being tested under difficult circumstances. Influenza had struck the community and four nuns were dying at about the time Léonie and Thérèse were exchanging letters. The stress of caring for the dying and the sick, adjusting to a new discipline of life, and grieving her father seems to have been too much for Léonie to bear.

Now we see more clearly the painful holocaust being asked of Léonie and its effect on her family. In our efforts to love God, we are not always blessed with success. It is possible to seem to have completely failed in the eyes of others. Even those very important to us might well judge us to be inadequate failures. This humiliation is crushing. Yet because we abandon ourselves to the fire of God's love as holocausts offerings, the Act of Oblation to Merciful Love extends even into difficult failure and humiliation. When we surrender ourselves as holocaust offerings through which His merciful love might be revealed, all the inadequacies and voids in our lives become the preferred places for this mysterious activity.

Some question whether it is wise to make such an offering. After all, who likes failure? Yet it is a mistake to think that this act of oblation causes failure. Instead, failure and humiliation are simply a painful part of life in this world. God moves hearts to make acts like The Act of Oblation to Merciful Love in order to dispose those whom He loves to offer up these difficult times for His glory rather than be overcome by them. To act when God prompts us to make such a holocaust offering of ourselves always leads to a deeper kind of obedience to His will.

Obedience in faith always opens up to a hidden fruitfulness. This is why Léonie and others who seemed to have failed in their efforts to follow God have a special place in the mission of the Church. The holocaust offering that they make of themselves reminds us that God is not so impressed with our spiritual accomplishments, but instead with our total surrender to His loving will—especially in failure and weakness. Through such radical vulnerability to God, we grow in the image and likeness of Christ Crucified. The more hidden under the shadow of humiliation, the more they are like Him in their love: a love fruitful and pleasing to the Father.

There are some who believe that the proper life of faith is magical, filled only with blessings, and devoid of failures and hardship. They even presume that if misfortune falls on a person of faith, it is because of a lack of character or weakness or some other defect. The logic of the Oblation to Merciful Love and the insight that difficult crosses are "a certain mark" of God's tenderness should incline us to rethink this assumption. What if human weakness and failure were not something that faith is meant to avoid or overcome, but instead, the very mystery in which faith finds God revealed?

St. Thérèse recognizes this kind of faith in her uncle during his visit. The treasure of his niece's religious vocation was taken from him and the public humiliation of her failure is given to him in return. His resignation and calm are remarkable, and Thérèse identifies this as a source of strength for the whole family. She understands that rather than being overcome, her uncle is choosing to believe and to trust in God and His secret purpose.

In the logic of Thérèse's Oblation, trust in the midst of trial unlocks the floodgates of divine tenderness. Abraham was credited with righteousness because he believed in the promises of God. It was his trust that allowed God to begin something beautiful in the history of salvation. This is the same trust of Mary's yes to the Lord. It is a decision to believe that God's providence is greater than the power of difficult circumstances to crush us. Because of the very nature of faith itself, St. Thérèse understands her sister's failure and her uncle's humiliation not as obstacles to faith, but as trials that lead to holiness.

Day 16—A Love That Possesses

Even before Thérèse completed this letter, Léonie came to the convent with her cousin Marie. Her uncle, after taking Léonie from the Visitation Sisters, went on a pilgrimage but sent Marie and Léonie back to Lisieux. Léonie wept while her sisters and her cousin comforted her. The strength that they had received because of their uncle's faith now gave them what they needed to console their sister and help her find her courage again. Faith makes space in our hearts for both sorrow and joy until we learn to offer both of these to the Lord in prayer.

DAY 17

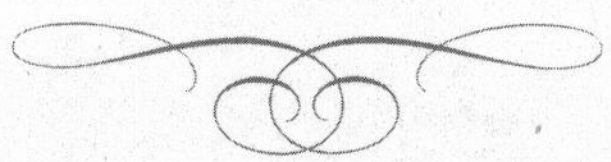

From Thérèse to Sr. Marie of the Trinity May 7, 1896.

THE AFFECTION [for the creature] is purely spiritual if the love of God grows when it grows, or if the love of God is remembered as often as the affection is remembered, or if the affection gives the soul a desire for God—if by growing in one, the soul grows also in the other.

He who walks in the love of God seeks neither his own gain nor his reward, but only to lose all things and himself for God; and this loss he judges to be his gain.

In the evening of life, they will examine you on love. Learn then to love God as He wills to be loved and forget yourself.

◆ ◆ ◆

St. Thérèse offered this encouragement on the day of Sr. Marie of the Trinity's religious profession. Sr. Marie had previous experience with the Carmelites in Paris and had lived a privileged life in many ways. She wanted to be a saint but others considered her too sensitive and emotionally needy. St. Thérèse had the role of forming novices like Sr. Marie and preparing them for their religious profession. She used her Act of Oblation and an approach to the spiritual life that she called "the Little Way" to help new members of the community become spiritually prepared for the sacrifices demanded by the Carmelite vocation.

This message that St. Thérèse wrote on the back of a holy card summarizes "the Little Way" through the counsels of St. John of the Cross. She provided this summary for a very solemn purpose. She wanted Sr. Marie of the Trinity to become a saint and not to be discouraged by her own inadequacies. This did not mean withholding affection or closing herself off from friendship. Just the opposite: it meant living in a network of warm friendships that built up the life of the community. The secret to such a web of grace would be to invest herself in those relationships that helped her become more and more attached to Jesus and less attached to anything that could distract her from Him.

This purpose is highlighted all the more by the very mysterious and painful circumstances surrounding this message. After returning from the Holy Thursday vigil St. Thérèse had her first hemoptysis: it was midnight and completely dark in her cell when she began to cough. She was not sure whether it was blood that she had coughed up, but she thought it might be. Remarkably, this was a great consolation to her. On the Eve of Good Friday, she understood that the Lord might not only call her home but also invite her to make a more perfect offering of herself by joining her physical suffering to His suffering on the Cross.

Thérèse's suspicion of terminal illness did not disturb her peace. Instead, she promptly went to bed—excited that when she woke up in the morning she would confirm whether what she suspected was in fact true. Souls that have grown in spiritual maturity acquire a degree of indifference about such things. This is because they have rooted their existence in the will of God and completely trust that His providence always works for the good. As is evidenced by her Act of Oblation to God's Merciful Love and the whole way she had lived and counseled others, St. Thérèse's ability to commend herself to the Lord and rest that evening testifies to her total confidence in Him. In the morning light, she awoke and saw that her handkerchief was in fact red with blood. This filled her with great consolation. She had wanted to live a short life and now she felt that the Lord had given her a small sign that her prayer would be granted.

Her awareness of her terminal illness precedes the spiritual trial that she was about to undergo. This spiritual trial began, however, not on Good Friday with her illness, but instead on Easter Sunday. Until she had this spiritual trial, she did not believe that those who had lost their faith really did not believe in God or heaven. Indeed, in French Catholic society as she knew it, it was inconceivable that anyone who lost their faith was being anything other than disingenuous. She assumed that the unbeliever's basic stance in life was one of obstinate self-contradiction. She had also assumed that this misery could be freely walked away from at any time. All it took, she thought, was simply accepting the mercy of God. She was not wrong, but she really did not understand or empathize with the suffering of these souls. In her own experience, the whole reality of God's love and the goodness of heaven was so obviously present she could never have imagined questioning it or understand why anyone would want to live without it. For these reasons, she never completely grasped the full complexity of the soul afflicted by a lack of faith. Her spiritual trial would change all of this.

St. Thérèse describes this trial as a veil descending. The thought of heaven was no longer consoling. She did not doubt the existence of heaven; instead, this doubt was existential—a reality related to her own finality. She could not conceive of how it could ever be possible to actually enjoy heaven in a personal and fulfilling way. It was a crisis of faith over whether she would ever find ultimate happiness in the promises of God for her own soul. Her spiritual pain was immense. She felt in the very core of her being that God had abandoned her. Remarkably, her love for God was not diminished and her faith in Him was not surrendered. But she was suffering the inner anguish that those who do not know God suffer in relation to their own happiness. She grappled with the apparent meaninglessness and absurdity of life that they, too confront, and with them, struggled to live bereft of the consolation of satisfying answers. Their questions became her questions and she felt solidarity with their plight. They were no longer strangers. She had always prayed for the unbelieving from afar, but as she prayed for them now, she prayed as one of them—even if they could not pray for themselves. She understood their doubts and their sense of alienation in a whole new light and became a channel of mercy by availing herself in this situation to the saving grace that they needed.

This annihilation of her spirit is analogous to the annihilation suffered by Jesus on the Cross. He became like us in all things but sin. This means that He also suffered the consequences of sin, including the experience of being alienated from His Father. Spiritual masters like St. John of the Cross insist that this was not an empty sacrifice for the Lord. To experience our disconnection from the Father was a true annihilation for the Lord—a real spiritual death—for the love and the blessing of the Father was the animating principle of His very life. To suffer the separation from God that is the result of our sin even for a moment would be for Him an oblation. However, He chose to offer up this separation not for a passing moment of His life, but unto death—allowing the total sacrifice of His humanity to become the definitive expression of His saving mission for our sakes.

The difference between our suffering and His is that our sin makes us deserving of punishment. He was blameless, yet He chose to embrace our fate because He could not bear to see us suffer alone. Out of devotion to the Father and to us, He freely entered into our misery and restored our dignity by standing in solidarity with us despite our sins. Thus, out of love, He truly meant what He prayed when He called out, "My God, my God, why have you forsaken me?"

St. John of the Cross expresses exasperation with those who consider themselves friends of the Lord but who will not embrace His total oblation of love for us by imitating it themselves. They are friends when prayer is consoling and gratefully embrace practices that they feel provide good mental hygiene. The prayer that Jesus offered from the Cross, however, they keep at a distance. They are afraid of what such an offering might mean for their own lives. St. John of the Cross wonders just what kind of friendship such attitudes allow (see *Ascent to Mount Carmel*, Book 2, Chapter 7).

It is into this very mystery of friendship with Christ, in solidarity with His salvific mission, that St. Thérèse has entered. She wants Sr. Marie of the Trinity to follow her. This kind of sacrificial love is not cold or indifferent to the suffering of others. It is not above human vulnerability or tenderness. Instead, it is plunged into the ache of our humanity and allows itself to be completely consumed by the love of God—not as experienced, but as hoped for. Such solidarity with Christ Crucified convinces us that our hope will not disappoint.

DAY 18

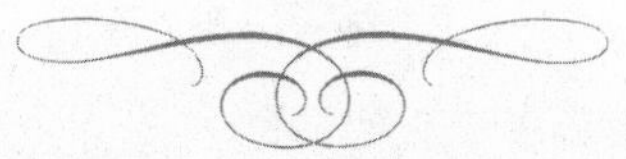

From Thérèse to Sr. Marie of the Sacred Heart September 13, 1896

Without showing Himself, without making His voice heard, Jesus teaches me in secret. It is not by means of books, for I do not understand what I am reading, but at times a word like this one that I drew out at the end of prayer (after having remained in silence and aridity) comes to console me: "Here is the Master I am giving you; He will teach you all you must do. I want to have you read in the book of life wherein is contained the science of Love." The science of Love, oh! yes, this word resounds sweetly in the ear of my soul. I desire only this science. Having given all my riches for it, I look upon this as having given nothing, just as the spouse in the sacred canticles. . . . I understand so well that it is only love that can make us pleasing to God, that this love is the only good that I ambition. Jesus is pleased to show me the only road which leads to this divine furnace, and this road is the *abandonment* of the little child who sleeps without fear in his Father's arms. . . .

"*Offer to God sacrifices of praise and thanksgiving*." See, then, all that Jesus is asking from us. He has no need of our works but only of our *love*, for this same God, who declares He has no need to tell us if He is hungry, did not hesitate *to beg* for a little water from the Samaritan woman. He was thirsty. . . . But when He said: "Give me to drink," it was the *love* of His poor creatures that the Creator of the universe was asking for. He was thirsty for love. . . . Ah! I feel it more than ever, Jesus is *parched*; He meets with only the ungrateful and indifferent among His disciples of the world and among His *own disciples* He finds, alas! few hearts that give themselves to Him without any reservations, that understand all the tenderness if His infinite Love. Dear Sister, how blessed we are to understand the intimate secrets of our Spouse. Ah! if you were willing to write all that you know about them, we would have beautiful pages to read, but I know that you prefer to keep in the bottom of your heart "the secrets of the King."

◆ ◆ ◆

There is a science of love that we learn only in the Book of Life. Jesus is "the way, the truth, and the life" (Jn 14:6). He is mysteriously present in the whole of our lives. His presence in our lives, especially in the midst of suffering, is hidden, unfamiliar, and hard to accept. There are wonderful joys in life, but there are also bitter sorrows. Contemplative prayer is open to both and allows Christ to draw us from one to the other. He does not permit us to suffer dark aridity except when He has something very beautiful to teach us in it: the science, the knowledge, of a deeper and more wonderful love.

This is why dryness in prayer is so important. Spiritual aridity feels like separation from God, but it is truly a deeper experience of His presence. Such spiritual hardship may cause us to question almost everything that we assume about ourselves and about the way that God works. In this dark ambiguity, we are not alone. Jesus Himself is teaching us in ways we cannot see or feel, or even remotely understand.

To know the truth is to know what is ultimate reality. What is ultimate, however, is above our limited understanding and exceeds anything we can imagine. The ground of all our experience and even our existence itself is much more than we can feel and always remains completely inaccessible to our intuition. Yet God Himself has revealed to us the answer to the riddle of who we are and gives us as a pure gift the truth that we could never grasp on our own.

To say that Jesus teaches us this truth in secret means that He offers a gift that exceeds our own power to understand. This means that the soul experiences this divine secret in aridity, without any feeling that He is close at hand. This is exactly the kind of contemplation that has become the daily bread of St. Thérèse. In it, divine love is fashioning her whole existence into a holocaust, a complete and total sacrificial offering to God.

What does the Lord teach us in the painful aridity of contemplative prayer? In this sacred silence when we think we are wasting our time, He discloses a truth that can only be known in the secret sorrows of life and of prayer. He whispers into the ear of our hearts powerful words that the frail limits of human intelligence cannot heed. This is what St. Thérèse identifies as the mysterious "science of love." It is a penetration of divine love into the deepest center of the soul and it renews everything! Christ Himself reveals that we are meant to acquire this wisdom when He declares, "I no longer call you slaves . . . but friends, for everything I have heard from the Father, I have made known to you" (Jn 15:15).

To know this science of love is to be open to the grace of a deeper trust and abandonment to God. It is a pathway to greater and greater confidence in the primacy of God's mercy over all the circumstances and troubles of our lives. The more progress we make, the greater our confidence becomes, and the more the transformative power of God's love burns in our existence. It is this fire into which we entrust ourselves when we take up St. Thérèse's Oblation to the Merciful Love of God. Immersed in these flames, divine light and warmth permeate our relationships and life circumstances. We do not see or feel, but the love of God is seen and felt by those He sends to us in all the ways that they most need it.

◆ ◆ ◆

The wisdom that St. Thérèse shares in this letter culminates in this insight. It is an insight that already animates the Oblation to Merciful Love written the year before. But now in the midst of her spiritual trial, she understands the movement of Christ's heart entrusted to her in a deeper and more intense way. Before her trial, she was already aware of this ache in the depths of Jesus, but now this spiritual trial has allowed her to enter into an even deeper and more fruitful union with the stirrings of merciful love.

Because she knows this movement of divine love in her own prayer—because she recognizes it in the daily circumstances of her humble life—she is able to convey a wisdom that would otherwise remain hidden. She knows, not as an idea but as a movement of her own soul, that the Lord is not indifferent to our ingratitude and indifference. It makes His heart ache when His love for us is not returned or returned in only a lukewarm manner. This intense and deep movement in the heart of Christ animates the heart of St. Thérèse's contemplation.

This thirst in the heart of Jesus is the deep secret of St. Thérèse's life of prayer. She shares it because she wants Sr. Marie of the Sacred Heart, her oldest natural sister and the first to enter Carmel, to understand why the Little Way is the best way to live out the Oblation to Merciful Love. To choose the Little Way is to choose to live moment-by-moment by and for love, to put as much love as we can in the moment that God has given us. This choice to live by love is motivated by the thirst of Christ. It seeks to alleviate the parched thirst of Jesus for our love by making every effort to love in the present moment. Like a sip of water offered to the parched lips of our Lord, this humble effort is nothing more than a wholly simple movement of love by faith hidden in the everyday circumstances of our lives. To live like this is to keep "the secrets of the King" at the bottom of our hearts.

DAY 19

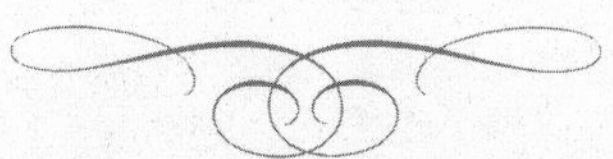

From Thérèse to Sister Marie of the Sacred Heart September 17, 1896

Oh, dear Sister, I beg you, understand your little girl, understand that to love Jesus, to be His *victim of love*, the weaker one is, without desires or virtues, the more suited one is for the workings of this consuming and transforming Love. . . . The *desire* alone to be a victim suffices, but we must consent to remain always poor and without strength, and this is the difficulty, for: "The truly poor in spirit, where do we find him? You must look for him from afar," said the psalmist. . . . He does not say that you must look for him among great souls, but "from afar," that is to say in *lowliness*, in *nothingness*. . . . Ah! let us remain then *very far* from all that sparkles, let us love our littleness, let us love to feel nothing, then we shall be poor in spirit and Jesus will come to look for us, and *however far* we may be, He will transform us in flames of love. . . . Oh! how I would like to be able to make you understand what I feel! . . . It is confidence and nothing but confidence that must lead us to Love. . . . Does not fear lead to Justice (1)? . . . Since we see the *way*, let us run together. Yes, I feel it, Jesus wills to give us the same graces, He wills to give us His heaven *gratuitously*.

Oh, dear little Sister, if you do not understand me, it is because you are too great a soul . . . or rather it is because I am explaining myself poorly, for I am sure that God would not give you the desire to be POS-

SESSED by *Him*, by His *Merciful Love* if He were not reserving this favor for you . . . or rather He has already given it to you, since you have given yourself to *Him*, since you *desire* to be consumed by *Him*, and since God never gives desires that He cannot realize. . . .

(1) To *strict justice* such as it is portrayed for sinners, but not this *Justice* that Jesus will have toward those who love Him.[1]

◆ ◆ ◆

This letter and yesterday's are part of what is known as Manuscript B of *Story of a Soul*. Sr. Marie of the Sacred Heart is again the designee. These letters were meant to help her understand why the Act of Oblation was so important and what it meant to live it out in daily life. Sr. Marie of the Sacred Heart has come to desire to be completely possessed by the merciful love of God. She embraces the purpose of the Oblation to the Merciful Love of God "to love God better for those who do not want to love Him."

Sr. Marie of the Sacred Heart was the third person, after Thérèse and her sister Céline, to make this offering. As a victim of merciful love, she has come to understand that offering and living out the Oblation of St. Thérèse means putting as much love as one possibly can into each moment until one completely lives by love—and even dies by love. This letter answers a very important concern that she had and that you have probably wondered about. Namely, how can any one of us live by love very long when we are so weak and prone to failure?

The answer that St. Thérèse offers is pure brilliance. It is possible to make a complete offering of ourselves to God's merciful love not because of our own greatness and spiritual industry, but because of our lowli-

[1] A note added by Thérèse. In the text she had crossed out "to Justice." This addition could have been made subsequent to the letter: its more careful penmanship contrasts with that of the lines: "Nine o' clock is ringing" down to the word "heart," words almost unformed.

ness. It is called the Little Way because this offering involves embracing our littleness and inadequacy. It requires that we humbly recognize that we cannot know with certitude whether we have made a good judgment about a situation before us, or what to do about it, or even how to pray about it. More than this, the Little Way makes us aware that we are oftentimes mistaken about what is really at stake in the heat of a moment and that many times we are unable to do the right thing. But with this awareness, we trust that God is working all things out for the good of those who love Him, and thus, for our good too.

This is not a matter of being passive, but of persevering with love and devotion in what we believe is the right thing, and doing so with the humble awareness that we are in constant need of the mercy of God. His "grace is sufficient" and His "power is made perfect in weakness" (2 Cor 12:9). If we are wrong, He already knows what is right; if we do not know what to do, He is already acting with power; and if we do not know how to pray, He is already teaching us to pray so as to be heard. We can trust in Him and proceed in love, even if we are mistaken, knowing that He is not mistaken. We can have every confidence that He will not allow us to stray too far. If we are wrong, He loves us so much that He will even use our mistakes for His glory. The moment He helps us to see our error, we must be confident that He loves a contrite heart that is ready to humble itself and begin again. St. Thérèse helps us to see that we can truly accept and love our weaknesses when we realize that in our failures and inability, God is waiting to do something beautiful.

This is the pure freedom of God's love. He owes no one anything but loves to give gratuitously. To those who feel themselves struggling in the mire and grit of this world, He freely opens up the mystery of heaven now in this life by faith—and this is nothing compared to what He yearns to give in the life to come. Spiritual happiness, the blessedness of heaven, is not something that we earn by spiritual feats or by our determined attempts to please Him. It is a pure and undeserved gift. The true victim of merciful love is a soul whose every effort to love is infused with the humble realization that God loves to lift up the lowly because they are lowly and to feed the hungry because they hunger. This is the mystery into which St. Thérèse is plunged. The thought of heaven, which had once brought her so much consolation, now torments her. Yet, she also knows that she has not labored in vain. Instead, her encouragement to her sister is the expression of an invincible certitude and reveals that nothing in this life can separate us from the love of God.

DAY 20

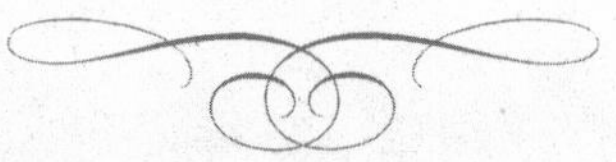

From Thérèse to Sr. Marie of St. Joseph
December 1896

How NAUGHTY to spend one's night in fretting, instead of falling asleep on the Heart of Jesus! . . .

If the night frightens the little child, if she complains at *not seeing* Him who is carrying her, let her *close her eyes*, let her *willingly* make the sacrifice that is asked of her, and then let her await sleep . . . when she keeps herself peaceful in this way, the night which she is no longer looking at will be unable to frighten her, and soon calm, if not joy, will be reborn in her little heart. . . .

Is it too much to ask the little child to close her eyes? . . . not to struggle against the chimeras of the night? . . . No, it is not too much, and the little child *will abandon herself*, she will believe that Jesus is carrying her, she will consent not to see Him and to leave far behind the empty fear of being unfaithful (a fear not fitting for a little child).

An Ambassador

◆ ◆ ◆

Sr. Marie of St. Joseph confided in St. Thérèse her fear of the dark. Our appreciation of St. Thérèse's answer remains only superficial if we presume that her fear was limited to the physical absence of light. There is a spiritual darkness that true prayer confronts. St. Thérèse is leading souls to live their lives as total spiritual offerings to the merciful love of God. This kind of sacrificial life requires entering into a prayer that we do not understand. It goes beyond everything that is familiar to us—and beyond us. Here, fear of the dark is more of a spiritual than physical reality and this short note attempts to address Sr. Marie's profound experience.

The merciful love of God is an immense mystery that overshadows our whole existence in constantly new and unfamiliar ways. Learning to accept the unfamiliar ways in which the Lord discloses His presence is necessary if our love for Him is to mature. Without this growth, we will be limited to offering ourselves to the Lord in ways that are familiar and comfortable to us—ways that in the beginning yield progress but in the end can become debilitating attachments. The more radical and complete gift to which St. Thérèse's Act of Oblation points challenges us to go beyond such limits.

Prayer that will not seek God beyond the consoling and therapeutic effects of His presence in our lives falls short of its goal. The purpose of prayer is not merely to attain what we think we need. Instead, prayer culminates in union with God in love. Such union is not like anything we have ever experienced or can imagine. To arrive at this total union with God that we do not yet know requires that we suffer all kinds of unfamiliar graces in prayer —secret workings of God that purify and intensify our humanity so that we can be more perfectly caught up in His tender mercy.

This radical confidence in God and courage in the face of His mysterious work is necessary for growth in spiritual maturity. When our conversation with the Lord does not produce the comforting sense of His presence or the feelings we expect, we are very vulnerable to all kinds of anxieties, distractions, and changes of mood. This is because in immature forms of prayer where we seek comforting and familiar graces, we limit God's communication with us. When we limit Him like this,

He cannot bring about the more complete purification of our hearts for which He yearns. It is only when we are submerged into a deeper prayer where God speaks to us in ways that we do not understand that we begin to recognize the monstrous ways we have limited God. We are shocked by our lack of faithfulness and wonder why God should continue to be faithful to us. This is the real fear that Sr. Mary of St. Joseph confronts and the reason why St. Thérèse is counseling her.

This does not mean that spiritual feelings or consoling insights are not useful when we begin to pray. God often lavishes us with these to encourage us to go deeper. At the same time, these graces are only a shadow of a prayer that is much more beautiful and fruitful. Sometimes, when the Lord believes we are ready, He takes this shadow away and overshadows us with His own presence. Thérèse calls this prayer "falling asleep in the Heart of Jesus." Sleeping in the Heart of Jesus requires that we do not become frightened by the darkness that accompanies this form of prayer. St. John of the Cross calls this overshadowing a "spiritual night" or "dark contemplation." In this kind of prayer, His transforming power is unleashed in the depths of our hearts and expands our capacity to love and to be pierced by the suffering of others. The more vulnerable we are to the plight of others and to the desires of God, the less vulnerable we are to various forms of self-torment or the passing of different emotional states in prayer.

St. Thérèse recognizes that the Lord has begun to lead Sr. Marie of St. Joseph into this transformative prayer. To enter into such prayer, one does not make efforts to avoid or overcome the darkness. Instead, like Mary who was overshadowed by the Most High, one simply assents to the mysterious work that God is accomplishing. When it is willingly offered, St. Thérèse calls this assent "abandonment."

DAY 21

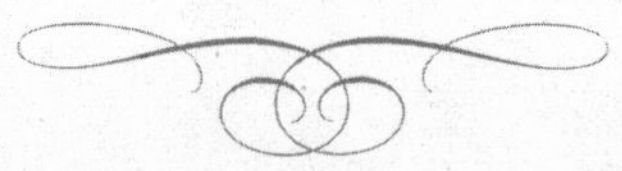

From Thérèse to Sr. Geneviève
December 24, 1896
The envelope is addressed: "Message from the Blessed Virgin to my dear Child without a home in a foreign land."

Dear little Daughter,

If only you knew how much you delight my heart and that of my little Jesus, oh, how happy you would be! . . . But you do not know, you do not see, and your soul is in sadness. I would like to console you, and if I do not do it, it is because I know the value of suffering and anguish of the heart. Oh, my dear child! if only you knew how my soul was plunged into bitterness when I saw my tender spouse St. Joseph coming back sadly to me without having found an inn.

If you want to bear in peace the trial of not pleasing yourself, you will give me a sweet home; true, you will suffer since you will be at the door of your house, but do not fear, the poorer you are the more Jesus will love you. He will go far, very far, in search of you, if at times you wander off a little. He prefers to see you hitting against the stones in the night than walking in broad daylight on a path bedecked with flowers that could retard your progress. I love you, oh, my Céline, I love you more than you could understand. . . .

I am delighted to see you desiring great things, and I am preparing still greater ones for you. . . . One day you will come with your

Thérèse into the beautiful heaven, you will take your place on the knees of my beloved Jesus, and I will also take you in my arms and will shower you with caresses, for I am you Mother, your dear Mamma.

Mary, Queen of little angels.

◆ ◆ ◆

In this letter, St. Thérèse writes to her sister Céline, Sr. Geneviève of the Holy Face, a message in the name of Mary, queen of "little angels." Who are the "little angels" over whom Mary exercises her queenship and what kind of queenship is it? To be *little*, to be considered of little consequence, to be taken by the world as someone of little significance: this is to have Mary, the Mother of God, as the queen of one's own spiritual life. Mary's Magnificat, her song before her cousin Elizabeth, celebrates the victory of the "lowly" and the "hungry" through the mighty power of God. As the handmaid whose lowliness is known by God, Mary, through her queenship, magnifies divine power in our lives. The Marian paradox reveals the way God prefers to work in both history and in our personal lives: divine power shines through human frailty to accomplish great things. St. Thérèse knows in the midst of her own trial of faith that to be little under Mary's queenship is to join her in magnifying and rejoicing in the superabundant greatness of the Lord. To help Sr. Geneviève embrace this same mystery and become its messenger through her own littleness, St. Thérèse identifies herself in the letter as "Mary, the Queen of little angels."

Sr. Geneviève has been offering the Act of Oblation to Merciful Love. She has faithfully lived out the Little Way on a daily basis. In this total offering of herself, her whole existence has been set ablaze by the fire of God's Love. She offers herself as a living sacrifice, not in outward ways, but through acts of love offered in holy secrecy and the hiddenness of authentic humility. This is the context in which Sr. Geneviève confronts a difficult sorrow. Her patience tried, she feels overwhelmed by her own inadequacy. We can imagine that she is approaching Christmas with a heavy heart, and it is into this deep sorrow that St. Thérèse offers a word of truth from the lips of Mary, the mother of our hope.

Ten years before, at the top of a flight of stairs in her home after Christmas Eve Mass, St. Thérèse had experienced the power of God's grace when it was least expected. Her father, when they got home, made a careless remark about the evening festivities about to take place. The remark crushed her spirit and her heart was ready to explode in a tantrum. It was in this very moment that she learned to make a sacrifice of praise, to turn a moment of righteous indignation into a moment of spiritual worship. She realized that she had a decision to abandon her sorrow to God and to choose to be joyful for her family, or to lose control of her emotions and rob the Lord of the freedom to do something beautiful.

In the grace of that Christmas Eve, the Little Flower chose to be little and to renounce her hurt pride. When she did so, she discovered, by the grace of God, the freedom to rejoice in His greatness. St. Thérèse recognizes that, in an analogous way, something of that same drama she had experienced is now haunting her sister. This letter, written in her own spiritual trial, is meant to be a cup of cold water offered to weary a pilgrim, a note of encouragement to help her sister choose what she herself had chosen.

St. Thérèse starts her letter by disclosing a powerful truth to Sr. Geneviève. Namely, that Sr. Geneviève is the heart's delight of the Baby Jesus and His Mother. Christianity is no impersonal religion. It is about intimate relationships and tender affection. We know the tender affection of the Son of God because of the hidden tenderness of Mary who welcomed Him into her womb. Mary, the Mother of the Christ-child, is also the mother who wants to console Sr. Geneviève, her "little angel." Mary is a source of great consolation in the life of prayer. Growth in mental prayer and the sacrifice of love that it makes possible requires suffering and sometimes very difficult and overwhelming trials. A soul that journeys this way becomes familiar with its own inadequacies and weaknesses. Sorrows do not magically go away when we offer ourselves completely to the merciful love of God. Instead, the Lord relieves us of the lesser sorrows we once carried so that there is space in our hearts to bear His sorrows with Him.

Mary knows this mystery. Because her soul has been pierced by a sword, as Simeon foretold, she knows how difficult suffering is for her "little angels" to bear. Just as she wanted to console St. Joseph, her spouse, when he could not find shelter for her, she also desires to console those who suffer rejection, hostility, and disappointment for her Son's sake. She is not indifferent, but she stands in solidarity with their littleness and beautifully consoles them in the ways that they most need when they most need consoling.

In addition to asserting the maternal love of Mary for her sister in her spiritual life, this letter also points out an important responsibility that Sr. Geneviève must embrace and reminds her of a key reason she must have confidence in the Lord during her present trial. The responsibility she has is to make her own heart a suitable home for Mary and Jesus. She can do this as she strives to be recollected in the merciful love of God and not overcome by sorrows that she confronts. The key reason for her to have confidence is that even when she fails (and she will), the Lord will not allow her to wander off too far. He is solicitous even as, in her efforts to love, she feels on the very brink of the limits of her own love and faithfulness. It is not because her own efforts will ever be enough, but because God's effort is more than enough, that she will be able to make a perfect offering to the Lord, one that reaches into heaven itself and opens up the gates of a deep and eternal communion of love. This devotion to the merciful love of God, rooted in a great trust in divine providence, is all Sr. Geneviève needs to be faithful in the total offering she is making of herself to the Lord.

DAY 22

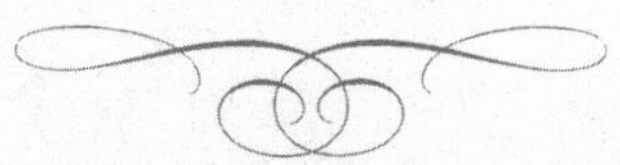

From Thérèse to Mother Agnes of Jesus
January 9, 1897

I HOPE to go soon up above. Since "if there is *a heaven, it is for me*," I shall be rich, I shall have all God's treasures, and He Himself will be *my good*, then I shall be able to return to you a hundredfold all I owe you. Oh, I am looking forward to it. . . . It troubles me so much to be always receiving without ever giving.

I would have liked not to have seen little Mother's tears flowing, but what I was happy *to see* was the good effect they produced, it was like magic. Ah, I am not vexed at anyone when my little Mother *is scowled at*, for I see only too well that the Sisters are merely instruments placed *in the way* by Jesus Himself so that *little* Mother's way (in *little* Thérèse's eyes) resembles the one He has chosen for Himself when He was a traveller on the earth of exile. . . . Then His face was as though hidden, no one recognized Him, He was an object of contempt. . . . Little Mother is not an object of contempt, but very few recognize her because Jesus has hidden her face! . . .

Oh, Mother, how beautiful is your lot! . . . It is truly worthy of *you*, the privileged one of our family, of you who show us the way just as the little swallow that we see always at the head of his companions, tracing out, in the air, the way that must lead them to their new homeland.

◆ ◆ ◆

Our homeland, the place where we finally are home, is a state of being not subject to this world but completely above it. This is not a matter of geography or physical space, but instead a matter of the very order by which God created all things. God created a cosmos of greater and lesser creatures and states of being. He placed spiritual and invisible realities over things that are tangible and visible so that things that can be seen and understood are subordinate and secondary to the mysteries of our faith. Heaven is one of these mysteries and as Christians we believe that it is our true home.

However, the world is not an evil to escape. The closer that Thérèse draws to death, the greater her appreciation for the goodness in this world, despite its painful misery. The goodness of the world, even when hidden in difficult trials, points to something above it, to a greater fullness, to a beauty that it cannot account for in itself. When those who ought to love us scowl, Thérèse understands that even this lack of appreciation is subordinate to a greater mystery—to the point of being an instrument of it. This is what Christianity understands when it proposes that heaven, our eternal destiny, is above this world.

St. Thérèse affirms the mystery of heaven in the midst of a crisis of faith. She attempts to provide her sister a heavenly perspective even as the very thought of heaven torments her. It is not that she does not believe in heaven, but that she finds herself unable to accept that she will personally enjoy this great mystery. It is over and against this struggle that she proposes to her sister that the trials of this world are subordinate to the mystery of heaven. She does this to provide a word of hope in the midst of difficult discouragement.

Sometimes as we strive to offer ourselves as living sacrifices to the Lord, difficult trials befall us and we become discouraged. In these moments, it is helpful to call to mind where and when our true consolation is found. Keeping heaven in mind helps us remember that we cannot take comfort in this world and that we will never find real rest in the present moment. These moments are only signs and instruments of something greater. They are at best a pledge of future glory, but not its realization. The true rest our spirits need is waiting for us in heaven above, where we are awaited by love. To arrive at this eternal love, we must go by the way eternal love has set forth for us: and this is the way of the Cross.

In heaven, the tenderness and kindness of God are known in an eternal communion that fulfills every desire with divine excess and fruitfulness. In this world, because of the evils that weigh down and oppress all that is genuinely human, God's tenderness and kindness take the form of a suffering love, a love that suffers all that has befallen those who are the special object of His divine solicitude. This suffering love—the expression of God's tenderness and kindness in the face of human suffering—is Divine Mercy, a merciful love from above that enters into the experience of humanity here below. Divine Mercy alone has the power to raise humanity above its earthly existence into a new kind of life—the eternal fullness of heaven. For St. Thérèse, even in her current trial, Divine Mercy is all-powerful and subjects everything to its sacred purpose. This means that everything in the world, every moment of our lives, can become a sign and instrument of Divine Mercy if we bind ourselves to suffering love by faith. Without grace, the human soul cannot recognize the signs that point to its true homeland, or take advantage of the devices by which it will make progress, or ever enter into the peace that it is meant to know. Without the help of grace, this life is simply too limited for the noble aspirations that live in the human heart. Yet, because of the inexhaustible mercy of God, grace flows out especially when humble souls realize their helplessness and cry out to the Lord in faith.

Those who offer themselves to the work of merciful love know that their resting place is in what is invisible and spiritual, present but not yet fully realized. On this earth, they are not at home, but instead they are exiles, pilgrims en route. Their journey is from what is here below to that which is above: from death and confusion to new life and truth. In this world, what is most beautiful and true is hidden; sometimes even completely eclipsed. The Act of Oblation to Merciful Love is offered not to surmount this reality, but in the very midst of its painful mystery. From the perspective of her spiritual trial, St. Thérèse understands this truth now more than ever. It is with this truth that she consoles her sister Pauline, or Mother Agnes, the former prioress of the Carmel in Lisieux.

Some might be surprised by the very human reality that politics can sometimes be intense in religious life. Pauline was elected prioress with the encouragement of Mother Marie of Gonzague. But Mother Marie of Gonzague was concerned about letting go of her firm control over the community. The young new prioress seemed sweet and timid and would likely accommodate her interventions, should they become necessary. If these were her plans, they did not come to fruition, for Mother Agnes was a very energetic and purposeful leader. Some of the sisters resented her leadership and Mother Marie of Gonzague was re-elected prioress. Mother Agnes humbly stepped down from her leadership position, even as her fellow nuns "scowled" at her. Into her sister's humiliation St. Thérèse directs her word of hope. She does not address her sister as someone who is above suffering. There are little phrases in this letter that preclude such an interpretation (". . . if there is a heaven" and "Jesus has hidden her face . . .").

St. Thérèse's spiritual trial was not fully appreciated until years after her death. Many looked on it as the result of an imperfection. They reckoned that God was still purifying her and that is why she experienced Jesus as "hidden" as she approached her death. Their assumption was that those who are purified always have a consoling awareness of the presence of God and if this consolation is not given, it is only because God is at work helping to bring it about. According to this rubric, St. Thérèse's spiritual trial would indicate that her love was still being brought to perfection and that the trial faced by Mother Agnes was also for purification, because Pauline was too sensitive and vulnerable in the judgment of others. A great saint, it is presumed, is not sensitive to the scowls of others but instead remains unmoved in the face of humiliation. Yet, Christian perfection does not follow this pathway of emotional and spiritual indifference to the circumstances and people God has put into the world.

St. Thérèse's spiritual vision of the hardship her sister confronts opens up a completely different perspective: the saving perspective of the Cross. Her message is the fruit of the dark contemplation that she has embraced for the salvation of those who least know God's love and feel furthest from His mercy. She does not contradict the opinion of those who believe that any spiritual trials that a soul faces as it follows Jesus can be purifying. However, rather than seeing these trials as merely therapeutic moments before the healing love of God, St. Thérèse recasts them as transformative moments, moments when we deeply identify with Christ and are united more intensely with His salvific mission.

As opportunities not only for imitating Christ but also for being conformed to His Passion, the scowls of those we love are instrumental. God is working through those who misjudge us and who hold us in disdain. This absence of love directed towards us personally is a manifestation of the misery that afflicts us all: the painful absence of a love we expect. It is precisely this wound resulting from the hostility of those we count on that God has come to heal. His mercy is superabundant. It is not enough for Him to heal it on His own; rather, He has chosen to implicate Himself in this misery through those souls who are willing to suffer all kinds of injustice and difficulties for love of Him. His exceeding tenderness turns those who are hostile to us into instruments of our transformation in Christ so that those who are the victims of hostility might become special vessels of His merciful love. Faith knows that those who rashly judge us are instruments in the hand of the Divine Physician. Before this kind of faith and devotion, all resistance to His love becomes a sacred space for Him to reveal the victory of His love anew. This is why, when our love is not returned, we choose by the love of God to love and believe in Him anyway. He is able to use even animosity towards us to manifest His saving mission in an entirely new and unique manner.

Each encounter, every interaction, and all circumstances are opportunities for the merciful love of God. Against the tired-out cycles of confrontation and conflict in this world, the grace of God makes our lives unique. Through faith, He works in our lives—no matter how unnoticed and underappreciated He may be—manifesting His salvific power in a particular way that will never be seen on the earth again. We must surrender with trust to this mystery and offer ourselves, just like Mother Agnes and Thérèse did, into the fire of God's love by choosing to love when love seems impossible. Despite the hostility of those with whom we live and who sometimes do not understand us, the message of this letter echoes what St. John of the Cross counseled centuries before: "Where there is no love, put love, and you will draw out love."

DAY 23

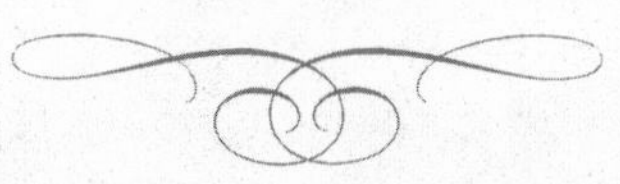

From Thérèse to Fr. Adolphe Roulland
May 1897

I KNOW one must be very pure to appear before the God of all Holiness, but I know, too, that the Lord is infinitely just; and it is this justice which frightens so many souls that is the object of my joy and confidence. To be just is not only to exercise severity in order to punish the guilty; it is also to recognize right intentions and to reward virtue. I expect as much from God's justice as from His mercy. It is because He is just that "He is compassionate and filled with gentleness, slow to punish, and abundant in mercy, for He knows our frailty, He remembers we are only dust. As a father has tenderness for his children, so the Lord has compassion on us!!" Oh, Brother, when hearing these beautiful and consoling words of the Prophet-King, how can we doubt that God will open the doors of His kingdom to His children who loved Him even to sacrificing all for Him, who have not only left their family and their country to make Him known and loved, but even desire to give their life for Him whom they love. . . . Jesus was very right in saying that there is no greater love than that! How would He allow Himself to be overcome in generosity? . . .

This is, Brother, what I think of God's justice; my way is all confidence and love. I do not understand souls who fear a Friend so tender. At times, when I am reading certain spiritual treatises in which perfection is shown through a thousand obstacles, surrounded by a crowd of illusions, my poor little mind quickly tires; I close the learned book that is breaking my head and drying up my heart, and I take up Holy Scripture. Then all seems luminous to me; a single word uncovers for my soul infinite horizons, perfection seems simple to me, I see it is sufficient to recognize one's nothingness and to abandon oneself as a child into God's arms. Leaving to great souls, to great minds the beautiful books I cannot understand, much less put into practice, I rejoice at being little since children alone and those who resemble them will be admitted to the heavenly banquet.

◆ ◆ ◆

The prayerful concern and deep admiration that St. Thérèse has for missionaries comes out in this letter. It is because of her intense solicitude for missionaries the Church has declared St. Thérèse a patroness of the foreign missions. The spiritual trial she suffers and the Act of Oblation that she is offering up through it are, in part, for their efforts. She participates in their work through her prayer. Pope Francis has asked for all the faithful to embrace missionary discipleship. This letter helps us see that the intercession of St. Thérèse and her spiritual wisdom are vital aids to this project. Her Act of Oblation is the secret to making our missionary discipleship fruitful just as it helped make the efforts of the missionaries in her own time fruitful.

Fr. Adolphe Roulland is a missionary priest in China. He has written a couple of letters in the last few weeks to report on his adventures and some successes in the mission field. His hope is that Thérèse will continue to pray for him. In fact, he views his successes as the result of her intercession and he needs her prayer to help him to persevere under very demanding physical circumstances. At the time, there was widespread hostility toward Europeans in China even as Father began his efforts. St. Thérèse has just learned that a missionary priest, ordained at the same time as Fr. Roulland, has been killed. She is aware that Fr. Roulland's life may also be in danger, and he is too. In a previous letter, he requests St. Thérèse's prayers for him, should he be killed, so that he might pass from purgatory to heaven. St. Thérèse reacts strongly to this request because of the lack of confidence in the mercy of God that he inadvertently discloses. In this letter, St. Thérèse encourages a new attitude toward divine justice, one rooted in trust in God's benevolence toward those who are doing His will. She also provides a hint as to where she has acquired the wisdom she is sharing with him.

To soothe Fr. Roulland's anxieties, St. Thérèse invites him to see the justice of God in a new way. Thérèse sees the Lord's perfect justice from the vantage point of her confidence in His goodness. She does not contradict the severity of divine justice, but she is also confident that God, in His justice, also knows our frailty. Speaking truth in the face of the anxieties of a young missionary who is attempting a very courageous and heroic ministry, she confidently asserts that God's justice and His mercy relate in a benevolent manner to our human condition. The merciful love of Christ Crucified does not permit us to assert otherwise. Therefore, rather than worrying over whether we measure up, we have every reason to trust that out of divine kindness, not only our failures but also our faithfulness are tenderly considered by God.

Where did this wisdom come from? The wisdom of St. Thérèse is a gift of prayer. Rooted in an unimpeded union with God, her heart is vulnerable to the gift of wisdom known by the Father and the Son. This movement of the Holy Spirit provides a soul with a taste for the Son's loving devotion to the Father and the Father's tender kindness to His Son. This Trinitarian vision instills the gravity of divine love in her teachings. Such wisdom is able to confront confusion and rash judgments about God and root our attitudes toward the Lord in better soil.

The word humility derives from the Latin *humus,* which means fertile soil. Our lowliness before the Lord is fertile when it is receptive to the great things that He wills to accomplish. Such receptivity characterizes the childlike confidence that St. Thérèse has in God. Put another way, the confidence of St. Thérèse is rooted in her humility, her utter reliance on God as if she were a child in His arms. Even in the midst of the difficult trial that she is currently suffering in her faith, this humility becomes the source of an unvanquished joy: "I rejoice at being little."

When it comes to understanding how God works in prayer, the childlike simplicity of St. Thérèse gives primacy to the Holy Bible. It can be a mistake to take a theological text into prayer. We grasp for a method or technique, a how-to manual, because we are afraid to be totally confident in the Father. Compounding our fears, few theologians research and write on their knees. Our theological effort is rarely open to the horizons of divine immensity that St. Thérèse sees. How can such theology be an aid to prayer if it was not born in prayer? When we take such research into prayer, our efforts to untangle elaborate doctrinal explanations can actually distract us from God rather than lead us into a deeper encounter with Him. To enter into the beautiful silence in which God instructs a soul, a simpler approach to prayer is needed.

For St. Thérèse, engaging with the Bible in prayer opens up "infinite horizons" because she trusts that the Sacred Scriptures are a reliable witness to God's Word. Her trust is rightly founded because the words of Holy Writ not only tell us about God and what He has done, but that the teachings of the Bible bear the Word of God Himself. We ponder the sacred doctrine of the Holy Bible not as an end in itself, but as a means to encounter Christ more deeply. The Sacred Scriptures can do this because, inspired by the Holy Spirit, they bear witness to the Son and the Father without error.

St. Thérèse has discovered what great Christian mystics have known throughout the history of the Church: the Bible, as the Church entrusts it to us in her tradition, contains everything that a soul needs to know about prayer. The teachings of the saints and doctors of the Church are all footnotes to what God has already revealed. Their wisdom, including the wisdom of St. Thérèse, is preserved to help us receive the teachings of the Holy Bible in the same way that they did so that we, too, might become saints. Contemporary authors are only good insofar as they refer us back to this same divine wisdom, insofar as they help us rediscover a living encounter with God that encourages holiness of life.

We gained access to this wisdom of holiness when the Father spoke to us through His Son. What His Son has revealed the Church remembers in her Tradition through the words of the Sacred Scriptures. Under the guidance of the Holy Spirit, our silent prayer truly accesses this living memory of the Church through the Bible and Tradition.

In her own efforts in the silence of Carmel, St. Thérèse found herself bathed in the light of God's word. In this light, she is able to propose to the young French priest a truth that we too must rediscover. From her prayerful reading of the Holy Bible she has learned that the heights of sanctity are not elaborate and distant, but simple and close at hand: "Perfection seems simple . . . it is sufficient to recognize one's nothingness and to abandon oneself as a child into God's arms."

This counsel "to recognize one's nothingness and to abandon oneself as a child" is a summary of her Little Way. Today, this summary is just as important for us as it was for Fr. Roulland. He was a missionary in a hostile country; we are missionary disciples in a hostile culture. The native people that he worked with harbored animosity towards Europeans. The culturally powerful of our own societies have instigated a dangerous climate for Christians around the world. If the Little Way of St. Thérèse with its movement of recognition and abandonment helped missionaries find courage in her own day, we should consider this same wisdom for our times.

This double movement of recognition and abandonment to the love of God lives at the heart of the Act of Oblation to Merciful Love. Conversely, without recognizing our littleness and abandoning ourselves into God's arms, it is impossible to make this offering of self to God's tender kindness. Offering ourselves to the Mercy of God depends on and deepens our awareness of our own littleness and our total surrender into His arms. The Act of Oblation can become a secret source of courage for missionary disciples to embrace this double movement in their own efforts to bring the Gospel of Christ into the public square.

Yet, our humble offering, with its simple movements of recognition and abandonment makes us vulnerable to new outpourings of God's tenderness and kindness in mysterious and superabundant ways. These outpourings not only benefit our own work and that of those immediately around us; they are outpourings that benefit the whole Church. Like a beat of the heart, such a pulse of life flowing through the Mystical Body can animate the work of all missionary disciples, no matter the difficulties and hardships they face.

DAY 24

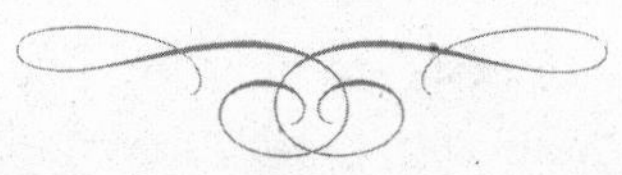

From Thérèse to Mother Agnes of Jesus
May 28, 1897

Dear little Mother, your little girl has again shed sweet tears just now, tears of repentance but more so of gratitude and love. . . . Ah! this evening I showed my *virtue* my *treasures* of *patience*! . . . And I who preach so well to others! I am happy you saw my imperfection. Ah, the good it does me for having been bad! . . . You did not scold your little girl, nevertheless, she deserved it; but your little girl is accustomed to this, your gentleness speaks more to her than severe words; you are the image of God's *mercy* for her. Yes, but . . . Sr. St. John the Baptist, on the contrary, is *usually* the image of God's *severity*. Well, I just met her, and instead of passing coldly by my side, she embraced me, saying: (absolutely as though I had been the best girl in the world), "Poor little Sister, I felt sorry for you, I do not want to tire you out, I was wrong, etc., etc. . ." I, who felt contrition in my heart, was astonished at her for not reproaching me in any way. I know that basically she must find me imperfect; it is because she believes I am going to die that she has spoken this way to me, but it does not matter, I heard only gentle and tender words coming from her mouth, and I found her very good and myself very bad. . . . When reentering our cell, I was wondering what Jesus was thinking of me, and immediately I recalled these words He addressed one day to the adulterous woman: "Has no one condemned you?" And I, tears in my eyes, answered Him: "No one, Lord. . . . Neither my little

Mother, image of Your tenderness, nor Sr. St. John the Baptist, image of your justice, and I really feel I can go in peace, for You will not condemn me either! . . ."

Little Mother, Jesus does well to hide Himself, to talk to me only from time to time, and "through the lattices" (Canticle of Canticles), for I feel I would be unable to bear any more, my heart would break, being powerless to contain so much joy. . . . Ah! you, the sweet Echo of my soul, you will understand that this evening the vessel of divine Mercy overflowed for me!

◆ ◆ ◆

The Christian life is not lived in a vacuum. Instead, our real communion together is a source of all kinds of trials and hardships, consolations and joys, sorrows and moments of humiliation. The drama of merciful love flows through a whole multitude of different encounters and surprising situations, in moments when we are strong and in those moments when we have been pushed beyond our limits. Perfection in this life does not consist of never making mistakes, but of constantly turning back to love.

St. Thérèse realized this perfecting mystery of mercy through the diverse personalities bound together in her own cloistered community. Each nun reveals some aspect of God so that their communion realizes the salvific paradoxes in this mystery. Purposefully and self-aware, or unwittingly and unaware, all of the sisters together are part of God's hidden self-disclosure for one another and for the world. This is as true for Mother Agnes, whom Thérèse calls "Echo of my soul," "image of God's mercy," and "little Mother," as it is for Sr. St. John the Baptist, "image of God's severity."

Sr. St. John the Baptist was in charge of the convent's linen closet. She was very suspicious of St. Thérèse and seems never to have been convinced of her sanctity. From the vantage point of the linen closet, she could see the novices going in for their formation meetings with St. Thérèse. Sometimes, she would even burst in on them and contrive a reason for having done so. Thérèse, in keeping with her Act of Oblation and the discipline of the Little Way, would patiently bear with this. But now St. Thérèse is growing more and more physically weak, spiritually tested, and emotionally fragile. This makes it increasingly difficult for her to patiently bear the weaknesses of her fellow religious and even the most normal difficulties that can emerge. This letter seems to address a moment of failure on the part of St. Thérèse, a moment when she lost her patience and had been reduced to tears.

Patience is an important virtue in the spiritual life. It regulates sorrow so that this emotion does not weigh down our existence, immobilize our will to do good, or prevent us from living for love. An impatient person is someone who is so overwhelmed with sorrow that they are no longer able to control themselves in their relationships with others. Without patience, sorrow can cause a soul to turn in on itself and become completely disconnected from others and from life. Without patience, such sorrow leads to despair. With patience, a soul may struggle with great sorrow, but in this struggle it never surrenders completely or gives up. Patience makes it possible to be unvanquished in our effort to love even in the midst of crushing personal failures and humiliations.

Christian faith does not take away sorrow, but it does open up the heart to bear it with the strength of Christ. Faith in Christ makes sorrow into a beatitude—a state of blessedness—because in union with Christ we are vulnerable to both the movements of His sorrow "unto death" and His deep joy "which no one shall take from you" (Mt 26:38, Jn 16:22). Why do we find blessing and joy in the midst of sorrow? Why can St. Thérèse claim in the midst of all her trials and sorrows that she knows so much joy she is not able to bear it? With the strength and patience that comes from the Lord, we, like Thérèse, can bear all kinds of difficulties and hardships because our patience does not come from ourselves; it is a gift from God.

St. Thérèse is being faithful to her Act of Oblation in the midst of this current trial by choosing to believe in God's mercy despite her failure. Because of this, she is amazed by the compassion (albeit imperfect) of Sr. St. John. Notice that Thérèse is not naïve about Sr. St. John. She knows that her compassion is occasioned by nothing more than pity. Pitying a dying person is not the same as esteeming them. Aware that this is the case, Thérèse chooses instead to marvel at the good that she sees in Sr. St. John. Although Sr. St. John only pities her, for St. Thérèse "it does not matter." She even uses the goodness she sees in Sr. St. John to humble herself and consider her own imperfections.

The perfection of the Christian life does not mean that we never fail in our efforts to love. Quite the opposite: to follow the footsteps of our Crucified Lord means being pushed beyond what we can handle on our own. Although God never leads us into temptation, He allows us to suffer all kinds of trials so that our lives might participate in and even extend His saving mystery in the world—not only through our successes, but especially through our failures. When we fall short, Christian perfection is already anticipated by our hope in God's readiness to raise us up and carry us to victory.

Christian perfection is realized by removing obstacles to God's love with the strength He gives us to do so. As we attempt to remove these obstacles, we are constantly made aware of our inadequacies. God works with us to remove obstacles to His love, but He does not always remove our weaknesses. The closer we draw to His love, the more we see how lowly and impoverished we are. Our posture becomes one of not just contrition, but adoration. When our efforts to be faithful to Him suddenly take their proper place, we find the freedom to surrender our pride, our programs for self-improvement, and our need to prove anything at all. Instead, our souls are bent in hushed reverence and gratitude.

Such vulnerability to awe and wonder gives God space to act with great power. He delights in transforming our limitations and failures. This is why He longs for us to offer to Him our misery the same way St. Thérèse humbly offered her own impatience to the Lord. In our own weakness, His strength is revealed.

The Act of Oblation, although it seeks to offer a perfect act of love, does not require perfection. The Little Way does not require that we pretend that people are nicer than they are or that we are better than we are. Instead, it requires that we accept others for who they are and ourselves in our own powerlessness. When we are mindful of how much we need the Lord, this awareness inclines us to regard the weaknesses of others with enough compassion that we are also able to marvel at the good God is accomplishing through them. This disposition makes space for Christ to come and visit us when we most need Him to communicate the saving truths that set us free.

DAY 25

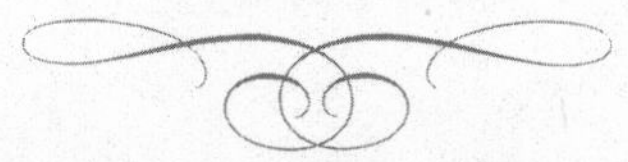

From Thérèse to Sr. Martha of Jesus
June 1887

DEAR LITTLE SISTER, yes, I understood all. . . . I am begging Jesus to make the sun of His grace shine in your soul. Ah! do not fear to tell Him you *love Him, even without feeling it*. This is the way *to force* Jesus to help you, to carry you like a little child too feeble to walk.

It is a great trial to look on the *black* side, but this does not depend on you completely. Do what you *can*; detach your heart from the *worries* of this earth, and above all from creatures, and then be sure Jesus will do the *rest*. He will be unable to allow you to fall into the dreaded *mire*. . . . Be consoled, dear little Sister, in heaven you will no *longer take a dark view of everything* but a *very bright* view. . . . Yes, everything will be decked out in the divine *brightness* of our Spouse. The Lily of the valleys. *Together* we shall follow Him everywhere He goes . . . Ah! let us profit from the *short moment* of life . . . *together* let us please Jesus, let us save souls for Him by our sacrifices. . . . Above all, let us be *little*, so little that everybody may *trample* us underfoot, without our even having the appearance of feeling it and suffering from it. . . . See you soon, dear little Sister; I take delight in seeing you. . . .

◆ ◆ ◆

We do not know the exact circumstances surrounding this letter. Sr. Martha, one of the novices entrusted to Thérèse, is in a deep spiritual darkness (the "black side") and struggling against falling into some kind of sin (mire). In the logic of the Act of Oblation and the Little Way, St. Thérèse directs her to the primacy of God's love. This perspective invites Sr. Martha into a posture of confidence despite her feelings. To encourage this confidence, St. Thérèse offers a remarkable piece of advice on how to *force* Jesus to help.

Strictly speaking, no one ever forces God to do anything. In the order of love, however, it is possible to make a kind of infallible appeal. The appeal is infallible because it is rooted in God's own tender kindness and Christ's promise, "Whatever you ask in my name, that I will do" (Jn 14:13). The Church has discerned the conditions of this promise to include that the petition must be made in faith, the request must be for a good necessary for one's own salvation, and, finally, one must ask with perseverance. Tradition considers this an infallible prayer.

Thérèse's counsel meets the criteria for an infallible prayer. She presents being carried by Jesus "like a child" as a grace necessary for our salvation. She invites a special response of faith: "Tell Him that you love Him, even without feeling it." She also encourages Sr. Martha to persevere in this petition by doing what she can. In particular, this means not giving in to worry and anxiety, especially when nothing seems to make sense.

Notice that St. Thérèse does not promise her that there will be any lasting consolation on this side of heaven. Thérèse's message is rather that Christ will carry Sr. Martha in the current darkness that has enveloped her. Though there will always be enough to keep going, she will not really have lasting light until she enters into the light of heaven. Instead, in this life, persevering in telling Christ we love Him means remaining little. This is a great paradox: our freely embraced littleness is what allows the omnipotence of God to act for our sakes.

To be little means not worrying or being anxious about protecting one's self or fearing what others might do or think. Rather than trying to defend oneself or allowing our own righteous indignation about an offense to fester, to be little means allowing Christ Himself to carry us through such trials. He will help us remain silent rather than complain or lash out in desperate efforts of self-preservation.

This littleness emerges when we entrust ourselves to God and His goodness rather than frantically relying on our own industry to preserve our dignity. Our effort is to offer ourselves to the Holy Spirit and to allow the Holy Spirit to teach us how to have compassion and intercede for those who have set themselves against us. When we are trampled underfoot by them, they need not know that we have suffered or felt anything.

To be detached in the way that St. Thérèse is recommending requires that we do not worry about what others think about us, especially if we want the freedom to show Christ how much we love Him. It is so often our attachment to things and others' opinions that keeps us in a darkness that the Lord would rather we did not experience. Insofar as we are affected by how others see us, we are not free to perfectly follow our Crucified Lord, who is divine brightness.

While there is outright abusive behavior that we are morally obliged to resist and to protect others from, there are other more insignificant forms of mistreatment that sting our pride and provoke us to lash out. In these situations, Thérèse's wisdom helps us remember that if God wants those who have overlooked us or mistreated us to know the suffering that they have caused, we must be confident that He will reveal this to them in His own way and in His own time. Only with this kind of trust—uninhibited by concern for ourselves—are we completely free to make known to Christ how much we love Him even when we feel no love in our hearts.

"He will do the rest."

It is precisely when others trample over us in our efforts to love God that Christ is carrying us. We have already entered into a beatitude that is above everything in this world. An immense joy is unfolding though we cannot see it. Our souls have developed a new solidarity with the Lord even as nothing else around us makes sense. His light is already dawning in this "short moment of life" and perfecting the holocaust that we offer of ourselves to Him: "Blessed are you when men revile you, insult you and speak falsely against you for my name's sake" (Mt 5:11).

Day 26

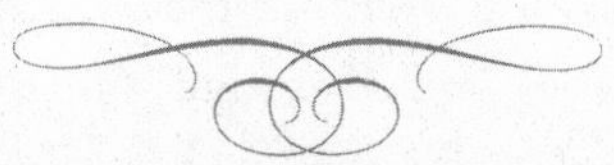

From Thérèse to Sr. Geneviève
June 7, 1897

Beloved little Sister, let us never speak what appears great in the eyes of creatures. Solomon, the wisest king who ever was on earth, having considered the different works that occupy men under the sun, painting, sculpture, all the arts, understood that *all* these *things* were *subject* to *envy*; he cried out that they were only vanity and affliction of spirit! . . .

The only thing that is not *envied* is the last place; there is, then, only this *last place* which is not vanity and affliction of spirit. . . .

However, "the way of man is not within his power," and we surprise ourselves at times by desiring what sparkles. So let us line up humbly among the imperfect, let us esteem ourselves as *little souls* whom God must sustain at each moment. When He sees we are very much convinced of our nothingness, He extends His hand to us. If we still wish to attempt doing something *great* even under the pretext of zeal, Good Jesus leaves us all alone. "But when I said: 'My foot has stumbled,' Your mercy, Lord, strengthened me! . . ." Yes, it suffices to humble oneself, to bear with one's imperfections. This is real sanctity! Let us take each other by the hand, dear little sister, and let us run to the last place . . . no one will come to dispute with us over it. . . .

◆ ◆ ◆

This note was occasioned by Sr. Geneviève after Céline sought a picture of her dying sister and novice mistress. Thérèse is so weak she cannot remain still for the photo which in those days took a while to take. Céline, the artist of the Martin family, seems to have gotten frustrated during this process. As a Carmelite Novice under the care of St. Thérèse, she is being formed in the Little Way and has been living out the Oblation to Merciful Love for almost two years. In this message, St. Thérèse's concern is not the fact that her sister became frustrated or even that her sister is a perfectionist. Instead, she is concerned that Céline has not yet fully accepted her own weakness.

Learning to prefer being powerless rather than having power in situations is a difficult interior mortification—that is, a death to self that no one else sees and that we often do not know is being accomplished in us. There is only so much that we can do so that ignoble dispositions do not gain the upper hand in our efforts to love one another. When we have done our part, then we need to humbly accept our own inner poverty and need for God to accomplish the rest. This difficult surrender is an interior mortification that puts to death the hubris by which we presume that our misery is something we can handle on our own terms and with our own internal resources.

The mystery of death provides an irreplaceable opportunity for this mortification, and here St. Thérèse's physical weakness has provided the occasion for this very painful spiritual need in the heart of Sr. Geneviève to surface. When someone we love is approaching death, we often attempt to gain control or do something about our own powerlessness. Our frantic efforts seldom produce good fruit. The Act of Oblation to Merciful Love is open to the Christian answer to this particular part of the sting of death. St. Thérèse is helping Sr. Geneviève learn this difficult answer—an answer rooted deeply in the Carmelite tradition.

Day 26—Offering Our Imperfections Is Patience

St. John of the Cross, in *Ascent to Mount Carmel*, provides counsels to help souls make swift progress to union with God. By the end of Book I, he has established that spiritual nights are a great blessing to be sought, not avoided. In Chapter 13, he lays out how to seek this blessing and what a soul should do in order to enter into "the night of the senses." His counsels all concern practices that influence our inclinations away from grasping for our own satisfaction. This is so that we might be more disposed to the Lord's mysterious preferences. Like Thérèse's gentle correction in this letter, St. John of the Cross counsels seeking what is least. His reason for doing so is rooted in devotion to Christ and in imitation of Him.

St. John of the Cross is convinced that the more we are like Christ, the more we draw near to Him. Like attracts like. If we would prayerfully study the life of Christ we would discover that He never did anything except for the glory of God. If we are to be like Him in doing everything for the glory of God, we must renounce anything in our lives that is not purely for this purpose. It is to help us make this renunciation that St. John counsels us always to incline ourselves *not* to the best but to the least; to be inclined *not* to be considered great but least; and to be content to be, in fact, the least of all. This is completely consistent with St. Paul's admonition to imitate Christ in Philippians. Christ "did not count equality with God a thing to be grasped, but emptied himself, taking the form of a servant, being born in the likeness of men. And being found in human form he humbled himself and became obedient unto death, even death on a cross" (Phil 2:6–8).

St. Thérèse affirms this same doctrine in her letter but adds something very beautiful. She sees our efforts to surrender and renounce having things the way we would like as an opening to a singularly powerful grace. She claims that it is when we take up being least, when we seek and desire the last place, that Christ "extends His hand to us."

The hand of Christ is ready to lift us up when we place ourselves in the last place. By renouncing our propensity to put ourselves first and having our own way, we give space for Christ to have His way. When we identify with Him in His poverty and powerlessness, He is able to fill us with His riches and strength. He lifts us up higher than we could have ever lifted ourselves and honors us more than we might have been honored by our own industry.

On a very practical level, this means bearing with our own imperfections. An imperfection is different than a sin. With sin, some degree of free will is involved. An imperfection is often involuntary and reveals a propensity to act against love. Such imperfections are the result of sin—sometimes original sin, sometimes personal sin, and sometimes even the result of a sin that has been committed against us. In the end, we cannot overcome our imperfections by our own efforts precisely because they often are involuntary. In order to learn to bear our imperfections and allow Christ's healing love to transform them, we need Christ to extend "His hand" to us.

Because an imperfection always involves a disinclination to love or an absence of love that ought to be within our hearts but is not, taken together, these imperfections constitute the misery and inclination to sin that lives in our hearts. Christ has come to redeem us from this misery. In His great mercy, He has already borne not only our imperfections but our sins on the Cross. He is the one who provides the grace for us to bear with our imperfections and to offer them to Him out of love.

In many ways, making this offering of our imperfections expresses the essence of Christian patience and the Act of Oblation of Merciful Love. This is because the holocaust offering of self in the fire of God's love that the Oblation expresses places our imperfections under the infused virtue of patience. By the patience and strength that comes from God (the very hand Christ extends to us) we bear with the greatest of life's sorrows: our own brokenness and emptiness.

Indeed, in this offering of self, the fire of God's love transforms everything into itself, including our imperfections. Our foibles do not disappear and the rough parts of our personality do not magically go away when we make the offering. Instead, the less pleasing propensities that we struggle with are caught up in the love of God and instead of separating us from the Lord or providing a barrier for others in their own journey to the Lord, our imperfections are transformed into a new and remarkable means of grace—one in which the power of God is made perfect in our weakness.

DAY 27

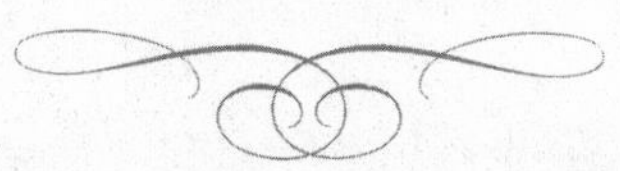

From Thérèse to Fr. Adolphe Roulland
July 14, 1897

When you receive this letter, no doubt I shall have left this earth. The Lord in His infinite mercy will have opened His kingdom to me, and I shall be able to draw from His treasures in order to grant them liberally to the souls who are dear to me. Believe, Brother, that your little sister will hold to her promises, and, her soul, freed from the weight of the mortal envelope, will joyfully fly toward the distant regions that you are evangelizing. Ah! Brother, I feel it, I shall be more useful to you in heaven than on earth, and it is with joy that I come to announce to you my coming entrance into that blessed city, sure that you will share my joy and will thank the Lord for giving me the means of helping you more effectively in your apostolic works.

I really count on not remaining inactive in heaven. My desire is to work still for the Church and for souls. I am asking God for this and I am certain He will answer me. Are not the angels continually occupied with us without their ever ceasing to see the divine Face and to lose themselves in the Ocean of Love without shores? Why would Jesus not allow me to imitate them?

Brother, you see that if I am leaving the field of battle already, it is not with the selfish desire of taking my rest. The thought of eternal beatitude hardly thrills my heart. For a long time, suffering has become my heaven here below, and I really have trouble in conceiving how I shall be able to acclimatize myself in a country where joy reigns without any mixture of sadness. Jesus will have to transform my soul and give it the capacity to rejoice, otherwise I shall not be able to put up with eternal delights.

What attracts me to the homeland of heaven is the Lord's call, the hope of loving Him finally as I have so much desired to love Him, and the thought that I shall be able to make Him loved by a multitude of souls who will bless Him eternally.

Brother, you will not have time to send me your messages for heaven, but I am guessing at them, and then you will only have to tell me them in a whisper, and I shall hear you, and I shall carry your messages faithfully to the Lord, to our Immaculate Mother, to the Angels, and to the Saints whom you love.

◆ ◆ ◆

St. Thérèse's illness is progressing rapidly and Fr. Adolphe Roulland has sent a letter in the hope that she might receive it before her death. Her response is not one of defeat and she does not have the attitude of someone whose efforts are drawing to a close. Just the opposite; she sees that, even as her earthly "envelope" is falling apart, her spiritual mission has only just begun.

Notice that the thought of beatitude "hardly thrills" her heart. This sentence suggests the terrible spiritual trial that she continues to suffer even as she offers these final words of encouragement to this young missionary. In the context of this letter, it also shows us something very powerful about the life of faith. The difficult trials that we face do not necessarily limit our ability to love and encourage one another.

It is true that suffering can cause us to turn inward and become self-occupied. It is true that terminal illness can at times cause us great anxiety and even push us to the brink of despair. In such suffering, one feels alone and withdrawn even from those whom one loves the most.

What is true of physical illness is even more so of a spiritual trial. Intense questions about our most fundamental beliefs take us into unbearable interior pain, as if our innermost self was being torn asunder and destroyed. Yet to feel as if one's whole life and being is engulfed in meaninglessness is not foreign to the mystery of our faith, and Christ's last wordless cry invites us to consider the radical extent to which He was willing to go so that we might not have to drink this cup alone.

When we offer our trials to the Lord as a sacrifice of love, the pain may remain and even become more intense, but it is endowed with new meaning. This new meaning comes to us through the agony suffered by Christ Crucified, whose self-offering infuses our own suffering with divine love. Because this love is stronger than death, suffering in faith does not limit us in the same way as suffering without faith—even when our faith is shrouded in darkness. Instead, offering to God our trials in prayer can increase our compassion for others and help us enter even more deeply into the drama of praying for them.

This is exactly what St. Thérèse exemplifies for us in this letter and it is the very basis of her spiritual mission. Just as in a holocaust offering where the victim is consumed by the sacred fire before the altar of God in the Old Testament, in the New Covenant we also offer ourselves as living sacrifices in the fire of God's love. The Act of Oblation to Merciful Love by which we are consumed in the fire of God's love does not end in this life, but continues in the next.

Here, in this life, our love on fire with God's own life is offered in suffering; there, our love burning in His is offered where suffering and sorrow are no more. Here, our efforts fall so short. There, God makes it so that what we will is perfectly realized. The Act of Oblation which seeks a single perfect act of love reaches for something that cannot be fulfilled in this life, but instead awaits us in the life to come. This is our hope, and this hope will not disappoint.

DAY 28

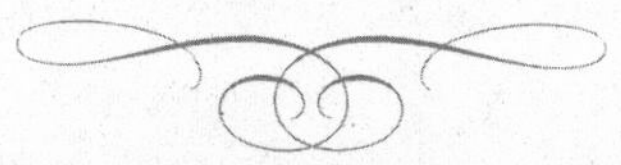

From Thérèse to Léonie, the last letter to her sister
July 17, 1897

Dear Léonie,

I am very happy to be able to speak with you again. A few days ago I was thinking I no longer had this consolation on earth, but God seemed willing to prolong my exile a little. I am not disturbed by it, for I would not want to enter heaven one minute earlier by my own will. The only happiness on earth is to apply oneself in always finding delightful the lot Jesus is giving us. Your lot is so beautiful, dear little sister; if you want to be a saint, this will be easy for you since at the bottom of your heart the world is nothing to you. You can, then, like us, occupy yourself with "the one thing necessary," that is to say: while you give yourself devotedly to exterior works, your purpose is *simple*: to please Jesus, to unite yourself more intimately to Him.

You want me to pray in heaven to the Sacred Heart for you. Be sure that I shall not forget to deliver your messages to Him and to ask all that will be necessary for you to become a *great saint*.

A Dieu, dear sister; I would like the thought of my entrance into heaven to fill you with gladness since I shall be able to love you even more.

Your little sister Thérèse

of the Child Jesus

◆ ◆ ◆

Unlike her sisters who have long settled into their vocations in Carmel, Léonie continues to struggle to understand her vocation and her life. Her family and many family friends are embarrassed for her. Others see her as weak and inadequate. She has many reasons to be discouraged. Yet, in the face of all of her failures and humiliations, she wants to be a saint. Although the secret greatness of Léonie is disguised in failed aspirations, in this last message written in her own hand, St. Thérèse conveys a deep sense of solidarity and profound confidence in her. She also makes a promise to help Léonie realize her deepest heart's desire not only in this life but the next. The love in which this promise is made is an example of a special kind of holiness that the world needs today.

We live in a culture where everyone needs to be successful. We are assured over and over again that the secret of happiness is not to fail. Prove to the world that you can achieve what you set out to do, and you have reached your full potential. When you can surmount your limitations and leave human weakness by the wayside, then you will finally arrive at greatness. Thus, rather than making our industry serve humanity, we have come to worship the work of our hands: our accomplishments, our achievements—these are the gods we serve. A self-sufficient and self-reliant world does not need to be loved by God. Grasping for control and accomplishment, it is incapable of genuinely connecting, heart to heart. So it grows old and stagnant, disconnected in the cold darkness of its own success. Those who choose this merciless state of existence do not freely live but merely exist diminished, in the shadow of the glory they were meant to know, self-content in a learned cleverness by which they put at bay the dull pain of an empty and meaningless life.

In the Christian tradition, the gift of holiness, a sheer grace, consists in love: allowing ourselves to be loved by God and sharing this love with those who most need it. Indeed, God's love is the sole source of new life, the animating principle of all that is genuinely human. This merciful love tenderly opens up the possibility of reaching beyond our self-occupation with our own successes and failures, and being free to enter into the story of our neighbor, to implicate ourselves in his or her plight, to do or say something that helps them remember the truth about who they are and the dignity with which they are endowed.

True holiness is not afraid of associating with the lowly. The holiness that comes from following Christ Crucified drinks deeply from the cup of human misery because it cannot bear the thought that someone might suffer alone. This Christian holiness has the capacity to enter into the heart of another, to listen until one's neighbor feels truly heard and understood. Such sacred love wonders over God's kindliness in the midst of human failure, and His power to raise up those completely cast down. Such a consecrating virtue is even capable of bearing all kinds of humiliation and heartbreak with invincible confidence because it is fixed in the certitude of divine providence. This love of God which tenderly animates our human love sees vast horizons of hope even in the face of death.

As her own death draws closer, rather than feeling stronger in her faith and enjoying a greater sense of spiritual accomplishment, St. Thérèse finds Léonie a source of consolation even as the saint struggles with all kinds of humiliating weaknesses—from gluttony to pride. It is in the midst of weakness that St. Thérèse finds a communion of failure, of inadequacy, but also of holy desire for God. The paradoxical awareness of their own littleness and their desire for holiness binds them together in a love stronger than death. Just as Mary rejoiced in what God achieves among the lowly and powerless, Léonie has become an instrument of consolation for St. Thérèse in the midst of her overwhelming trial. The love of God at work in her gives her confidence that she will be able to help her sister from heaven—even as she struggles to believe in the possibility of her own beatitude.

The example of St. Thérèse is an example for all those who aspire to become missionary disciples in the world today. It was not because she was successful that she was able to help her sister, but because she was vulnerable to her sister's heartache. It was not because her faith was free of difficulties that she found solidarity with her sister, but because her faith was tested. It was not because she had overcome her weaknesses that divine love bound her to her sister, but because she continually offered her imperfections to God. In all of this we begin to understand that not success, but humble faithfulness makes our Act of Oblation to Merciful Love a beautiful sacrifice to God

DAY 29

From Thérèse to Fr. Maurice Belliere
July 18, 1897

AH! HOW I would like to make you understand the tenderness of the Heart of Jesus, what He expects from you. In your letter of the 14th, you made my heart thrill sweetly; I understood more than ever the degree to which your soul is sister to my own, since it is called to raise itself to God by the *elevator* of love and not to climb the rough *stairway* of fear. . . . I am not surprised in any way that the practice of familiarity with Jesus seems to you a little difficult to realize; we cannot reach it in one day, but I am sure that I shall help you much more to walk by this delightful way when I shall have been delivered from my mortal envelope, and soon, like St. Augustine, you will say: "Love is the weight that draws me."

I would like to try to make you understand by means of a very simple comparison how much Jesus loves even imperfect souls who confide in Him:

I picture a father who has two children, mischievous and disobedient, and when he comes to punish them, he sees one of them who trembles and gets away from him in terror, having, however, in the bottom of his heart the feeling that he deserves to be punished; and his brother, on the contrary, throws himself into his father's arms, saying that he is sorry for having caused him any trouble, that he loves him, and to prove it he will be good from now on, and if this child asks his father *to punish* him with a *kiss*, I do not believe that the heart of the happy father could resist the filial confidence of his child, whose sincerity and love he knows. He realizes, however, that more than once his son will fall into the same faults, but he is prepared to pardon him always, if his son always takes him by his heart. . . . I say nothing to you about the first child, dear little Brother, you must know whether his father can love him as much and treat him with the same indulgence as the other. . . .

But why speak to you of the life of confidence and love? I explain myself so poorly that I must wait for heaven in order to converse with you about this happy life. What I wanted to do today was to console you.

◆ ◆ ◆

The seminary formation of Fr. Maurice Belliere was less than perfect and now he is beginning his mission to Africa. He has been entrusted to St. Thérèse and so even though she is nearing the end of her strength, she is completely committed to supporting him and his work of evangelization. Although he is a little idealistic, he had struggled with his vocation and, at one point, even fell into serious sin. Now he is attempting to do something beautiful for God, but St. Thérèse knows that he needs a better approach and surer footing for the task ahead. In this summary of the Little Way, we see St. Thérèse catechizing a missionary priest on how to reach the heights of Christian perfection.

To live a good spiritual life, we need good spiritual doctrine. Poor spiritual teaching leaves us vulnerable to all kinds of inconstancies and anxieties. False or weak doctrine regarding the spiritual life fails to recognize that human evil is limited—even the evil of our own actions—and that only true spiritual teaching helps us discover that this limit is only found in the infinite horizons of merciful love.

We live in a time of great insecurity when many turn to self-help programs and techniques, but are afraid to turn to God with their emptiness. Christians feel out of control, so they look for psychological gimmicks and spiritual shortcuts that allow them to take control of their life circumstances. They have a sense that accumulating more things and grasping for more comforts is not the way forward, but they are afraid to let go of the works of their hands. They allow the things we make and enjoy to lay claim to our existence in ways for which they were never intended.

St. Thérèse is a Doctor of the Church precisely because her spiritual doctrine is not only good but fully relevant for our times. She directs us away from all impersonal efforts at self-improvement. She offers something much richer than the mental hygiene one might find through silent self-reflection. She does not propose a therapeutic approach to God. Instead, she invites us into personal familiarity with the Lord. She proposes a true personal relationship and an ongoing heart-to-heart conversation with Jesus.

Speaking into Fr. Belliere's insecurities over his lack of perfection and past failures, St. Thérèse is encouraging him toward a more personal and intimate encounter with the Lord. She wants him to be aware of Christ's presence that is not only with him, but for him. She invites him to deeper confidence in the Lord. She contrasts the way of fear with the way of love, just as a steep stairway contrasts with an elevator. To grow in a personal relationship with Jesus, progress is made, not by the long tired-out stairway of fear, but by a new divine invention: an elevator of love.

In her story, the confidence of the one son frees the father to be indulgent in the face of disobedience, while the lack of confidence in the father's goodness prevents him from showing his love. The relationship between the freedom of the father's love and the son's confidence is presented as analogous to the need for confidence in Divine Mercy in the face of sin. Confidence in God frees the Father to express His love and only His love can address the reality of sin—for the whole reality of sin is nothing more than the absence of a love that ought to be, but is not.

God who is Love can heal what is absent in our hearts, but He needs our confidence in His mercy in order to restore and save us.

The two mistakes that can be made when we are confronted with our own sinfulness are presumption and despair. In presumption, we never really look at the horrific void of love that we suffer or that is the cause of suffering in those around us. Because it is so painful and humbling to accept our misery and littleness before God's goodness, we are tempted to pretend that the empty meaninglessness we have introduced into our lives is not there. It is a great falsehood to believe that by being mindless about the suffering we have caused it magically goes away. What really happens, when sin is not dealt with, is that everyone around us becomes oppressed by the burden of our own guilt—those we most love have to deal with the ugliness we will not face.

To counter presumption, St. Thérèse proposes a personal relationship with Christ in which, with total confidence in His benevolence to us, we make ourselves completely vulnerable to His judgments and point of view about the decisions we have made. This kind of familiarity with Jesus in personal prayer opposes the magical thinking of presumption and the assumption that our own actions do not really count. Sincere and ongoing conversation with the Lord about the reality of our lives helps us see that presumption never builds anyone up but always oppresses and pulls others down. At the same time, the humble confidence we bring into this holy conversation with Christ does not allow the eyes of our hearts to be distracted from His loving gaze.

If St. Thérèse is not counseling presumption she is even more adamant that souls should avoid even the first movements of despair. In these movements, we become so overcome by remorse and regret over our failure, we lose sight of the mercy of God. Fascinated by the depths of our own depravity, we do not raise our eyes to the Father who awaits us with love and understanding. In despair, we deceive ourselves into thinking that our own wickedness is more powerful than God's goodness and understanding. We pull back from His merciful kindness and retreat into self-torment and demonic self-accusation.

Both despair and presumption ground a soul in pride. Defining ourselves on our own terms rather than receiving our identity from the One who made us in love, we refuse to serve Him either out of self-occupied fear or out of rash carelessness. As long as we refuse to humbly surrender to the Father in confidence, we prevent God from raising us up in His own humility. Only in the vast horizons of divine humility do human freedom and weakness find themselves baptized and raised up by the immensity of His love.

St. Thérèse of Lisieux opposes the fear that God cannot really deal with the absence of love that eats at our existence and she stands against any lack of confidence that His goodness really is triumphant over our misery. Her Little Way requires the courage of accepting our littleness and inadequacy, our inability to deal with our misery on our own. It requires the humility rooted in one's own identity as a son or daughter of God. Such humility not only takes responsibility for failure, but also constantly renews its devotion to God at every opportunity and in every moment. Thérèse's elevator of love demands confidence in the tender kindness of God to lift us up and to give us a new beginning.

The way of confidence and love is the secret of the Act of Oblation to Merciful Love, and the secret of being a successful missionary. Whether we are sent to Africa or to the house next door, the perfect act of love, this total holocaust of self, is not realized except through trust in divine goodness. It is perfected only in the fire of God's love. This is why the humility it requires before the immensity of God's tenderness opposes all efforts of self-justification. Instead, this decision to offer oneself completely to the Lord during this short life entrusted to us disposes us to trust instead of fear, and to fill the hearts of others with love instead of tormenting ourselves with unrepentant self-accusation.

DAY 30

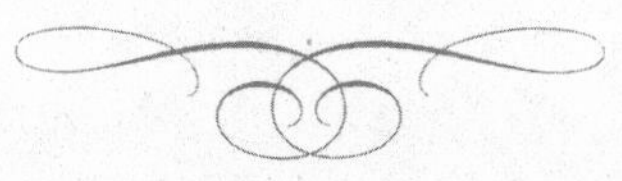

From Thérèse to Fr. Maurice Belliere
July 26, 1897

AH! YOUR SOUL is too great to be attached to any consolations here below. You must live in heaven by anticipation, for it is said: "Where your treasure is, there is you heart also." Is not *Jesus* your *only Treasure*? Since He is in heaven, it is there your heart must dwell, and I tell you very simply, dear little Brother, it seems to me it will be easier for you to live with Jesus when I shall be near him forever.

You must know me only imperfectly to fear that a detailed account of your faults may diminish the tenderness I have for your soul! Oh, Brother, believe it, I shall have no need "to place my hand on the lips of Jesus." He has forgotten your infidelities now for a long time; only your desires for perfection are present to give joy to His Heart. I beg you, do not *drag* yourself any longer to *His feet*; follow that "first impulse that draws you into His arms." That is where your place is, and I have learned, more so than in your other letters, that you are *forbidden* to go to heaven by any other way except that of your poor little sister.

I am in total agreement with your opinion: "The divine Heart is more saddened by the thousand little indelicacies of His friends than by even the grave sins that persons of the world commit"; but, dear little Brother, it seems to me that it is *only* when His own, unaware of their continual indelicacies, make a habit of them and do not ask His pardon, that Jesus can say these touching words which are placed for us in His mouth by the Church during Holy Week: "These wounds you see in my hands are the ones I received in the house of those who *loved me*!" Regarding those who *love* Him and who come after each indelicacy to ask His pardon by throwing themselves into His arms, Jesus is thrilled with joy. He says to His angels what the father of the prodigal son said to his servants: "Clothe him in his best robe, and place a ring on his finger, and let us rejoice." Ah! how little known are the *goodness*, the *merciful love* of Jesus, Brother! . . . It is true, to enjoy these treasures one must humble oneself, recognize one's nothingness, and that is what many souls do not want to do; but, little Brother, this is not the way you act, so the way of simple and loving confidence is really made for you.

◆ ◆ ◆

In order to know the goodness of the Lord, we must humbly recognize our littleness in the world. God is immense and His plan is immense, and our proper place before Him and in the grandeur of His work is quite humble. We are not above this world but in it. When our efforts are not offered for the glory of God, no amount of grasping for control or fighting for our rightful place or defending our own honor ever attains anything truly worthwhile. Yet, the humble effort to accept who we are before God and where we stand before Him takes more than our own industry can achieve. To become lowly and humble of heart, to become a true child of God, can only be realized by being confident in His great love in all circumstances and trials, and this even as we enter into the extreme powerlessness and humiliation of death (see Romans 8:12–13).

Death would seem to be the final humiliation of our humanity and the greatness for which we are called. Our bodies are living icons of the image and likeness of God, but death separates soul from body so that only a vestige of its former glory is left. Like the Holy Trinity, we are made for communion with one another but death alienates us from those to whom we are bound so that they see us no more. We are made to be fruitful, but death rends from our body its very fruitfulness so that all that we have achieved and accomplished is taken from us. At the same time, the last spark of our humanity when offered in faith realizes its nobility and sees a goodness that cannot pass away. Although hidden in disembodied powerlessness and cast down in the eyes of the world, all that is most unique and particular in the lowliness of those who render this last sacrifice of love remains treasured beyond all telling and tenderly awaited in the immensity of Divine Mercy.

It is to this mystery that St. Thérèse of Lisieux is directing her young missionary. She is compelling because she has already chosen this Little Way and followed it faithfully to its final end. Jesus did not choose to grasp for power, and so she chose to be powerless. Jesus did not seek security, so she chose to be vulnerable. The Blessed Trinity did not overwhelm humanity to gain its homage, so she chose to be little. She learned to welcome the unsurpassable gift offered through the humility of God by practicing humility herself. The holocaust she offered by confidently casting herself into the fire of divine love gives her the vantage point of contemplating God's goodness. She yearns for nothing else than that Fr. Belliere might discover this vantage point for himself and make it his own.

Fr. Belliere's story after the death of St. Thérèse is one of great suffering, misunderstanding, and rejection by his own community. While in Africa, he contracted sleeping sickness, a then-fatal illness that left him weak not only physically, but also mentally as it ran its course over a five-year period. Unable to faithfully persevere in his responsibilities as a priest he was sent home. His religious community came to believe that he had simply lost his mind for no apparent reason. Rejected and unable to fit into society, he became a beggar and lived homeless for a time. When someone finally found him, he was admitted into Bon Saveur in Caen, the same sanitarium that once treated St. Louis Martin, Thérèse's father. He died a month later.

He was buried in the cemetery of his family's parish church in Langrune just north of Caen. Until further study of these letters was undertaken, his life, and seemingly failed effort as a missionary, were considered insignificant, perhaps even an embarrassment. As devotion to St. Thérèse grew, however, so did questions about this mysterious priest, the exact nature of his failure, and the true meaning of his final suffering.

Thérèse's Act of Oblation sheds light on his life and the greatness of his dignity. She identified his path to salvation with her own—a Little Way of confidence, of seeing the goodness of God from the vantage point of lowliness. Her own witness throughout her final illness and spiritual trial allows us to ponder how she might have continued to guide and support her "little brother" in all his trials in finding the vantage point that she herself had found: the vantage point of being insignificant, lowly, and vulnerable before God. Just as St. Thérèse accepted a very difficult trial out of devotion to Christ, the mystery of Merciful Love seems to have permitted him also to suffer being broken both physically and mentally. We can only guess at the difficult spiritual trial into which this missionary priest had fallen. Completely misunderstood and misjudged, homeless and helpless, he had nothing else than the mercy of God and the spiritual help of St. Thérèse.

Those who have embraced the Little Way and made the Oblation of Merciful Love their own are convinced that his story does not reflect defeat or failure, but the fulfillment of St. Thérèse's promise to him: that he could go to Jesus by no other path than the Little Way she proposed to him. It is difficult not to notice in the passages she cites from his letter to her that he has been pierced to the heart by the heartache Christ has over our plight. Even as he wrote her, the movements of mercy were already carrying his soul. The Act of Oblation to the Merciful Love of God opens us up and disposes us to become channels of divine love in the world, oftentimes in ways we cannot understand.

If this is true, Fr. Belliere's apparent failure was not a failure at all, but a means by which the mercy of God has begun to flow into the world. If someone were to ask for proof that he truly participated in God's salvific work in a meaningful way, it would be difficult to provide on this side of eternity. In this world, we only see a small part of the story. Yet something about the story of this priest and the special role that St. Thérèse played in his life is compelling.

If you believe that St. Thérèse continued to help him after her own death and that she walked with him throughout his difficult trial, you might find it interesting that a grave marker now has been placed at the site of his burial. It reads, "Spiritual Brother and Protégé of St. Thérèse."

It is on this point of solidarity with St. Thérèse that we end these reflections on the Act of Oblation of Merciful Love. The total holocaust of self offered in the fire of God's love that she advocated is really a very simple movement of our hearts. It is a surrender and abandonment to Merciful Love, and an effort to generously welcome all the graces that everyone else has rejected. It is a Little Way by which we humble ourselves in the present moment for love and by love. Sometimes, when Divine Mercy leads us to the very limits of our human misery, it is not a movement we can make by ourselves but which requires the help of the whole Church, especially our brothers and sisters who have gone before us in faith.

All the hosts of heaven bind themselves to us in love, and by faith we are implicated in a whole communion of saints. They are all ready to apply their merits to our feeble efforts, and they do so knowing that everything they have merited to share with us is nothing more than a participation in what Christ has merited for once and for all. And among our heavenly friends who tirelessly intercede and support us in our own offering, St. Thérèse has a special place, especially for those who are struggling the most. She offers a Little Way and she is ready to walk along with us just as she has for countless spiritual brothers and sisters who have bound themselves to her by making the same Act of Oblation that she made of her own life—a total holocaust of self for the sake of a single perfect act of love.